THE TIMES
PICTURE COLLECTION
EXPLORERS

THE TIMES
PICTURE COLLECTION
EXPLORERS

Richard Sale
and
Madeleine Lewis

Collins
An Imprint of HarperCollinsPublishers

ISBN-10:0–00–714566–7
ISBN-13:978–0–00–714566–9

ISBN-10:0–06–081905–7 (in the United States)
ISBN-13:978–0–06–081905–7

Copyright © Times Books 2003
The Times is a registered trade mark of Times Newspapers Limited, a subsidiary of News International plc.

Designed by Colin Brown

Printed and bound in Italy by Editoriale Johnson

05 06 07 08 09
9 8 7 6 5 4 3 2 1

The publishers would like to thank: Sue Lawford, Alpine Club Photo Library; Pauline Hubner and Justin Hobson, Royal Geographical Society; Dick Bass; Lucy Martin, Scott Polar Research Institute; Erik Decamp; and particular thanks to Amanda Faber for all her work in the development stage of the project.

PICTURE CREDITS

All reasonable efforts have been made by the Publisher to trace the copyright holders of the photographs contained in this publication. In the event that a copyright holder of a photograph has not been traced, but comes forward after the publication of this edition, the Publishers will endeavour to rectify the position at the earliest opportunity. The Publishers are grateful to the following individuals and organisations for permission to reproduce their photographs.

2–3 RGS **5–9** Richard Sale **10** TNL **10–11** Scott Polar Research Institute, University of Cambridge **12** (top) National Maritime Museum, London (bottom) RGS **13** (top) Popperfoto (bottom) Richard Sale **14** (top) RGS (bottom) Richard Sale Collection **15** (top) RGS (bottom) Richard Sale Collection **16** Richard Sale **17** (top) Richard Sale Collection (middle & bottom) Fred Goldberg **18** (top) Susan Barr (bottom) Hulton Archive **19** (both) Arctic and Antarctic Museum, St Petersburg **20** Richard Sale Collection **20–21** Richard Sale **21** (right) Richard Sale Collection **22** RGS **23** Hulton Archive **24** (both) Danish Polar Centre **25** (top) Rune Gjeldnes/Torry Larsen (bottom) Per Michelsen **26** (top) Arctic and Antarctic Museum, St Petersburg (bottom) Richard Sale **27** (left) Richard Sale Collection (right) Chauncey Loomis **28** Richard Sale Collection **29** (top) Hulton Archive (bottom) Richard Sale Collection **30** Corbis **31** Swedish Polar Research Secretariat **32** Richard Sale Collection **33** Per Michelsen **34** (top) Richard Sale Collection (bottom) Byrd Polar Research Centre **35** (top) Hulton Archive (bottom) Richard Sale Collection **36** (left) Richard Sale Collection (right) Bettmann/Corbis **37** (top left & right) Swedish Polar Research Secretariat (bottom) Arctic and Antarctic Museum, St Petersburg **38** Børge Ousland **39** Canterbury Museum, New Zealand **40** Richard Sale Collection **41** (top) Richard Sale Collection (bottom) Canterbury Museum, New Zealand **42** (top) RGS (bottom) Scott Polar Research Institute, University of Cambridge **43** Mansell Collection/Timepix **44** (top) Swedish Polar Research Secretariat (bottom) Scott Polar Research Institute, University of Cambridge **45** (top) Hulton Archive (bottom) Richard Sale Collection **46** Richard Sale Collection **47** Hulton Archive **48** (top) Richard Sale Collection (bottom) Scott Polar Research Institute, University of Cambridge **49–50** S.A. Museum, South Australia **51** (both) Mitchell Library, State Library of New South Wales **52** (top) RGS (bottom) Richard Sale Collection **53** (top) Richard Sale Collection (bottom) New Zealand High Commission **54** (top) Canterbury Museum, New Zealand (bottom) TNL **55** Børge Ousland **56–57** Richard Sale **58** Corbis **59–60** Richard Sale Collection **61** (left) Topham Picturepoint (right) Richard Sale **62** Mountain Camera Archive **63** Richard Sale **64** Popperfoto **65** (left) Alpine Club Photo Library, London (right) Erik Decamp **66** John Cleare **67** John McDonald **68** John Cleare/Mountain Camera **69** Alpine Club Photo Library, London **70** Richard Sale Collection **71** (left) Richard Sale Collection (right) John Cleare/Mountain Camera **72–73** Colin Monteath/Mountain Camera **74** (left) Alpine Club Photo Library, London (right) RGS **75** (left) Richard Sale Collection (right) RGS **76** RGS **77** (top) RGS (bottom) Richard Sale Collection **78** (bottom) TNL **78–79** RGS **79** (bottom) TNL **80** TNL **81** RGS **82** Louis Lachenal **83** RGS **84** Richard Sale Collection **85** Hermann Buhl **86–87** Richard Sale Collection **88** TNL **89** Fritz Wintersteller **90** (top) TNL (bottom) Richard Sale **91** Hulton Archive **92** Dick Bass **93** David Hamilton/Mountain Camera **94** (both) Richard Sale **95** Byrd Polar Research Centre **96** Richard Sale Collection **97** John Cleare/Mountain Camera **98** David Hamilton/Mountain Camera **99** Colin Monteath/Mountain Camera **100** J Ramón Agirre **101** David Scott-Macnab/Mountain Camera **102–103** Sir Wilfred Thesiger/Pitt Rivers Museum, University of Oxford, permission granted courtesy of Curtis Brown **104** Hulton-Deutsch Collection/Corbis **105–106** RGS **107** (top) RGS (bottom left) Nigel Bean/naturepl.com (bottom right) John Sparks/naturepl.com **108–109** RGS **110** Mansell Collection/TimePix **111** (both) RGS **112–113** The British Library **114** Topham Picturepoint **115–116** RGS **117** (top) RGS (bottom) Hulton Archive **118** Hulton Archive **119** RGS **120** Sir Wilfred Thesiger/Pitt Rivers Museum, University of Oxford, permission granted courtesy of Curtis Brown **121** (both) TNL **122** RGS **123** Popperfoto **124** Sir Wilfred Thesiger/Pitt Rivers Museum, University of Oxford, permission granted courtesy of Curtis Brown **125–128** RGS **129** National Library of Australia **130** State Library of South Australia **131** National Library of Australia **132–133** RGS **134–135** Loren McIntyre **136–137** Hulton-Deutsch Collection/Corbis **138** RGS **139** (top) Popperfoto/Alan Greeley (bottom) by permission of Ray Hoole, great grandson of the photographer, Francis Harold Watson **140** (above) RGS (bottom) Hulton-Deutsch Collection/Corbis **141** Bath Royal Literary and Scientific Institution **142** Mansell Collection/TimePix **143** (left) Hulton Archive (right) Bettmann/Corbis **144** (left) Hulton Archive **144–145** RGS **146** (top) Bruce Davidson/naturepl.com (bottom) Hulton-Deutsch Collection/Corbis **147** (left) TNL (right) RGS **148** (top) RGS (bottom) Topham Picturepoint **149** (top) Mansell Collection/TimePix (centre, left) Bettmann/Corbis (centre, right) Hulton-Deutsch Collection/Corbis (bottom) Brown Brothers, Sterling, PA **150** (top) TNL (bottom) RGS **151** (top) TNL (bottom) Hulton-Deutsch Collection/Corbis **152** Anthony Fiala/National Geographic Image Collection **153** (left) Anthony Fiala/National Geographic Image Collection (right) RGS **154** (top left) RGS (top right) TNL (bottom) Hiram Bingham/National Geographic Image Collection **155** (top) Hiram Bingham/National Geographic Image Collection (left) Brown Brothers, Sterling, PA (right) South American Pictures/Tony Morrison **156–157** Corbis **158** Brown Brothers, Sterling, PA **159** D.H. Clarke/PPL **160** Barry Pickthall/PPL **161** Popperfoto **162** Topham Picturepoint **163–164** Popperfoto **165** (both) Associated Press **166** (left) Pelletier Micheline/Corbis Sygma (right) Flyer/PPL **167** (left) Popperfoto (right) Topham Picturepoint **168** (top) Popperfoto (bottom) Associated Press **169** Popperfoto **170** (both) Hulton Archive **171** (top) Tom Mclean Enterprises/PPL (centre) Popperfoto (bottom) Corbis **172** (top) Popperfoto (bottom) Associated Press **173** (top) Bettmann/Corbis (bottom) Associated Press **174–181** Chris Howes/Wild Places **182** (both) Bettmann/Corbis **183** Popperfoto **184** (both) Bettmann/Corbis **185** Hulton Archive **186–187** Popperfoto **front cover** Mawson Antarctic Collection, S.A. Museum **back cover** RGS

RGS = Royal Geographical Society, London
TNL = Times Newspapers Ltd

CONTENTS

Introduction

Man's early exploration of the world was carried out not to increase his knowledge of it, but to settle it, as population pressure forced people to migrate. Only slowly, over many thousands of years, did this change. Trade came to dominate in areas where the settled population represented a formidable challenge, whilst a thirst for plunder drove explorers to regions where more vulnerable civilisations were found. The impetus behind these journeys came from the kingdoms of Europe – although the Chinese had ocean-going junks, they abandoned long-distance seafaring in the late 15th century. As was said of the Portuguese, who under Dom Enrique (Henry the Navigator to the English-speaking world) began the great voyages of exploration, 'God gave them a small country as a cradle, but an entire world as a grave'.

The Spaniards, British, Dutch and others who followed the Portuguese may have been financed by kings and merchants driven by greed, but for some of the ordinary sailors on the ships, experiencing the hardships and dangers of medieval travel, but returning again and again to the sea, there was something more profound at work. For them exploration was an end in itself, challenge and discovery being as important as reward. They were the forerunners of the explorers to whom this book is dedicated, those who sought out untouched wildernesses – mountains, the poles, jungles, deserts and the worlds beneath the ground and sea – for the joy of doing so. Many then and now question why men do such foolhardy things. To answer that question would require a book of its own, but it is worth noting the words of Fridtjof Nansen, the foremost polar explorer of his generation, whose words apply equally to all those mentioned in the following pages:

'People, perhaps, still exist who believe that it is of no importance to explore the unknown polar regions. This, of course, shows ignorance. It is hardly necessary to mention here of what scientific importance it is that these regions should be thoroughly explored. The history of the human race is a continual struggle from darkness towards light. It is, therefore, to no purpose to discuss the use of knowledge: man wants to know, and when he ceases to do so, he is no longer man.'

Richard Sale, December 2002

Ice

Of the world's ice-bound territories, the Arctic was first settled thousands of years ago by Asiatic nomads moving north, then east across the Bering Sea land bridge which connected Asia and North America during the Ice Ages. Later, from the ninth century AD, came the Vikings. They were settlers, exploring the land in order to probe its assets, to weigh up its potential to support their families. The first people to map the Arctic came from northern Europe, just as the Vikings had. They were not driven by a search for land to settle, but by the commercial requirement to find an alternative route to the riches of the Orient, since by the 15th century the Spaniards and Portuguese were in control of the Atlantic.

From Britain came John Cabot, sailing north-westwards in May 1497, to be followed years later by Frobisher, Hudson and Baffin. In 1619, the Dane Jens Munk overwintered on the eastern shore of Hudson Bay, he and two others being the only survivors of a 65-man expedition. Later (in 1631),Thomas James was forced to overwinter in what is now James Bay: his book on the journey is widely believed to have inspired Coleridge to write *The Rime of the Ancient Mariner*.

By contrast to the Arctic, the Antarctic was discovered not by mapping the land, but by probing the ocean and so mapping where there was no land. In the north, men had expected to find ocean and in fact found land: in the south they expected to find a continent and saw only water. In 1642 the Dutchman Abel Tasman sailed around Australia, proving it was not part of a southern continent, and in the years that followed expeditions beyond latitude 50°S showed that the Southern Ocean was an empty place, pushing back the possible shores of the expected land mass. In 1578 Englishman Francis Drake was blown south to about 57°S, while another Englishman, George Shelvocke, reached 61°30'S during the austral summer of 1719–20. Shelvocke's book of his journey included an account of the shooting of an albatross. This was read by William Wordsworth who in turn suggested to his friend Samuel Taylor Coleridge that he use the incident in the epic poem he was then writing. Coleridge substituted a crossbow for the shotgun used by Shelvocke's man and used the killing as the central theme of *The Rime of the Ancient Mariner*. Both poles, therefore, can claim some credit for the work.

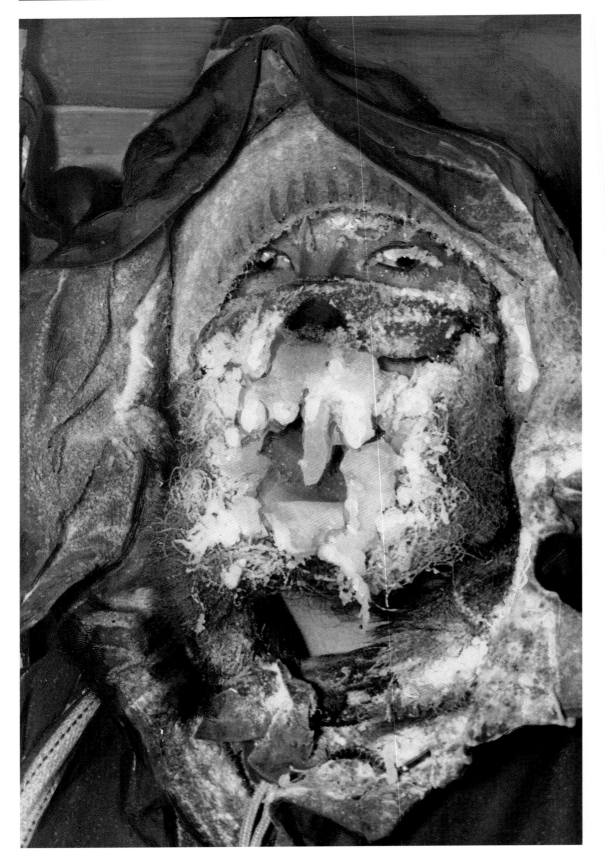

left
The popular image of
polar exploration is
exemplified by this photo
of Lt Angus Erskine, a
member of the British
North Greenland
Expedition which
surveyed the northern
island from 1952 to
1954. Lt Erskine was
caught in a blizzard.

THE NORTH-WEST PASSAGE

The quest for a North-West Passage, a navigable route westwards along the northern coast of the Americas to Asia, became something of a Holy Grail to early European explorers. After its early failures, Britain realised that the search for the Passage was futile and turned its attention to the land, ousting the French and setting up the Hudson's Bay Company to exploit the fur-bearing animals of the Arctic rim. A Company man, Samuel Hearne, followed the Coppermine River and Alexander Mackenzie went down the Mackenzie River and later became the first European to view the Pacific Ocean from the North American coast.

In the wake of the Napoleonic Wars, the quest for a North-West Passage was resurrected as a means of occupying Britain's large and temporarily redundant navy. Naval officers were sent on both land and sea journeys, filling in the gaps in the mapping of the northern coast of Canada. John Ross rediscovered Baffin Bay. William Edward Parry won a prize for becoming the first man to reach 110°W, overwintering successfully on Melville Island. On land John Franklin retraced Hearne's journey down the Coppermine. On later journeys Parry found the Fury and Hecla Strait, named for his ships, while Franklin retraced Mackenzie's journey, then turned west to reach Herschel Island. Here Franklin was stopped by bad weather: he was less than 250 kms (about 155 miles) from the most easterly point reached, Frederick Beechey heading east from the Pacific. Had Franklin met Beechey later history might have been changed.

Following the string of failures to find the Passage, or much else of great interest, the British public became apathetic about further attempts and naval expeditions ceased. Exploration did not. Hudson's Bay Company men continued to carry out valuable work. One was John Rae who proved that the Boothia Peninsula was part of the mainland, not an island as had been thought. In 1828 John Ross was engaged by Felix Booth, bottler of the famous gin (and for whom Boothia Peninsula is named), to have one more try to discover the Passage. Ross failed, but his young nephew, James Clark Ross, who accompanied him, reached the North Magnetic Pole.

Back in Britain the Admiralty, concerned that the relative success of private expeditions was making its own efforts look ridiculous, decided to try one more time. Looking around for a likely commander they discovered that all their Arctic men were either retired or disinclined. Only one man was willing, his willingness due in large part to the enthusiasm of his young wife Jane who wished to see her husband given the credit he was due for a long and distinguished career. Under Jane's relentless pressure the navy eventually gave in and appointed John Franklin to the command.

John Franklin's is one of the most famous names in Arctic exploration, his entry into history coinciding with the new art of photography. In 1845 Franklin took the *Terror* and *Erebus* west. They were spotted by a whaler in Baffin Bay but after that neither ship, nor Franklin or any of his 128 men, were ever seen alive again.

below

In the Arctic, explorers had to face the challenges of hostile terrain and climate. There was also the possibility of attack by polar bears, which are not just the world's largest but also the only truly carnivorous bears. The early explorers probably took a less relaxed attitude to that of these observers of a female and two cubs swimming off Greenland's north-eastern coast.

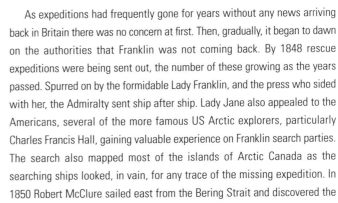

left
This early daguerreotype shows John Franklin at the time the expedition sailed. It shows an old and overweight man (he was almost 60) – not really the expected image of a man suited for command of an Arctic expedition lasting several years.

As expeditions had frequently gone for years without any news arriving back in Britain there was no concern at first. Then, gradually, it began to dawn on the authorities that Franklin was not coming back. By 1848 rescue expeditions were being sent out, the number of these growing as the years passed. Spurred on by the formidable Lady Franklin, and the press who sided with her, the Admiralty sent ship after ship. Lady Jane also appealed to the Americans, several of the more famous US Arctic explorers, particularly Charles Francis Hall, gaining valuable experience on Franklin search parties. The search also mapped most of the islands of Arctic Canada as the searching ships looked, in vain, for any trace of the missing expedition. In 1850 Robert McClure sailed east from the Bering Strait and discovered the northern passage, though he completed the crossing by sledge when his ships were iced in. Despite this, back in Britain McClure received a knighthood and, after much complaining, the reward for discovering the passage, a reward he declined to share either with his crew or his rescuers, a decision which appalled everyone except himself.

While McClure was searching in the east, the first trace of Franklin was found in the west where, on Beechey Island, three graves and a cairn of food were found. More than a century after they were buried the men who occupied the graves were exhumed and examined by a Canadian team. The men, their bodies perfectly preserved in the deep freeze of the permafrost, were shown to have died of natural causes but to have had high levels of lead in their systems which would have exacerbated any illness. It is conjectured that the expedition, one of the first

left
Dr John Rae in 1862. After the savagery of the attacks on him by British society and the press, Rae continued to explore in northern Canada making several important journeys. He died in London in 1893, aged 79. His wife took his body to the Orkneys where he had spent his childhood. He is buried behind St Magnus Cathedral in Kirkwall.

to use tinned food, had been poisoned by the lead of the solder which sealed the cans. Recently it has been suggested that the contents of the tins — poor-quality food prepared in distinctly unhygienic conditions — may have been contaminated, food poisoning further reducing the men's ability to overcome the rigours of the Arctic winter. But three graves and a pile of food tins did not solve the mystery of what had happened to Franklin. The Admiralty had by now lost half-a-dozen ships and were becoming weary of the effort. Franklin had been gone six years and no one except Lady Franklin thought he was alive. Quietly they shelved plans for further rescue attempts, though Lady Jane continued to finance her own search.

In 1853 John Rae, the Hudson's Bay Company man, led a land expedition in search of Franklin, finding Inuit who told him of a large group of white men who had been seen heading south along King William Island's western shore. The men had been exhausted and reduced to cannibalism by extreme hunger. None had survived.

left
Amundsen's ship *Gjøa*, now preserved in Oslo outside the museum which has been constructed over Fram. The ship is surprisingly small considering the epic nature of the journey through the North-West Passage.

above
Sir Francis McClintock. Despite confirming Rae's story about the fate of Franklin, McClintock did rather better out of the tragedy. He was knighted, promoted to Admiral, made a freeman of the city of London, given several honorary degrees, a gold medal by the Royal Geographical Society and a fat reward. He is also mentioned below Franklin's bust in Westminster Abbey.

right
There is little doubt that Amundsen was the greatest of all polar explorers: first man to the South Pole; probably among the first to see the North Pole; first through the NW Passage; second west-east transit of the NE Passage; first overwinter in Antarctica. Yet for all his achievements he remains an enigmatic man, to whom the Norwegians never took to as they did to Nansen. Amundsen became increasingly embittered as he grew older, feeling that the fame he was due was being unjustly withheld. He also did himself harm with an act which started out surprising everyone for its kindness. During the Maud expedition Amundsen rescued two young Chukchi girls from extreme poverty. Kakonita was motherless, dirty and lice-infested, while Camilla was of mixed race and consequently unwanted by her tribe. Amundsen took them to Oslo as foster children, offering them to be a home, security and an education. But eventually Amundsen grew tired of the girls and packed them off to Seattle for a return to Chukchi and an uncertain future. In fact the two settled in America and lived contented lives there, but that was no thanks to Amundsen.

above
The crew of *Gjøa* after the ship had reached Nome in Alaska. Amundsen is to the left.

Rae obtained from the Inuit relics which were clearly from the expedition. These, and the tale of lingering death and cannibalism, he brought to Britain. The reaction of officialdom and the press was outrage. The Times castigated Rae for believing the word of Inuit as they 'like all savages are liars'. Charles Dickens published articles in which he developed this theme and also insisted that no Englishman could possibly have stooped so low as even to contemplate cannibalism. Far more likely was that the Inuit had murdered Franklin's men, perhaps even eating them as well, and were now trying to shift the blame on to the innocent victims. Rae was condemned for having been duped. Despite his efforts in the Arctic, which included a very real claim to having discovered the southern North-West Passage (the route eventually followed by Amundsen), Rae never received the knighthood he rightly thought was his due.

Despite the controversy over Rae's discoveries, the Admiralty still refused to send another expedition, and Lady Jane, keener than ever to discover the truth, financed another, Francis McClintock sailing in 1857. After overwintering twice, McClintock's men finally found evidence suggesting Rae's tale was correct. All along the western shore of King William Island

The 5th Thule - Ekspedition 1921-24
The north west passage -
Knud Rasmussen

were the remains of Franklin's expedition, these including skeletons and ship's boats and, in a cairn, a note that said that Franklin had died in 1847 and that the two ships had been abandoned in the ice off the island. The surviving members of the expedition had headed south towards the Great Fish River which no doubt they hoped would lead them to a Hudson's Bay Company fort. King William Island is a desolate, unforgiving place. With food running low the exhausted men died along the way, the last of them dying after resorting to cannibalism. As a tale of horror and despair, long drawn out and hopeless, the Franklin expedition has few equals, even if the real story will never be known.

The British gave up any thoughts of completing the passage after Franklin. The country had been mapped; if it could be sailed at all the passage was not a commercially viable waterway. And so it was forgotten for half a century, until the 31-year-old Norwegian Roald Amundsen took up the challenge. Reasoning, correctly, that much of the problem with the British attempts had been the use of ships that were too big, he headed west in a small herring boat called *Gjøa* (pronounced you-ah) with a crew of seven. The Norwegians sailed through Lancaster Sound, then south through Peel Strait and around King William Island to winter in what is now Gjøahaven. After two winters there *Gjøa* sailed west to Herschel Island from where Amundsen sledged south to Eagle City to announce the news that he had successfully sailed the North-West Passage. Technically, of course, Amundsen was premature, *Gjøa* not actually completing the voyage until the following year when it rounded Point Barrow and sailed through the Bering Strait.

above
The first commercial transit of the North-West Passage. Escorted by the Canadian icebreaker *John A McDonald*, the 155,000-ton US tanker *Manhattan* made the transit in 1969 using the northern route. As the ice shrinks northward, a shrinkage which is consistent with, but does not prove, global warming, the possibility that the medieval dream of a commercial northern route from the Atlantic to the Pacific draws ever closer.

above top
In 1923–24 as part of the Fifth Thule Expedition (a series of journeys aimed at exploring Inuit culture as well as filling in final gaps in the Arctic maps) the Dane, Knud Rasmussen followed the Passage by land with dog sledges over the ice. This photo shows the returning sun after winter on the ice. Rasmussen's journey was repeated, solo, by the Japanese Naomi Uemura in 1974–76 and then in 1991–93 by a young Spaniard, Ramón Hernando de Larramendi.

left
Cape Dezhnev, the
easternmost point of
Asia. On top of the rise
is a lighthouse/memorial
to Semen Dezhnev. The
other buildings are said
to be research
accommodation, but
with Alaska just across
the Straits it is possible
they were also used for
more clandestine
operations.

THE NORTH-EAST PASSAGE

In the mid-16th century the discovery of a narwhal tusk on the shores of the Kara Sea, off Russia's northern coast, sparked interest in a north-eastern route to the Orient. As the toothed whale was unknown, the object was clearly a unicorn horn, and it was 'known' that 'Unycorns are bredde in the landes of Cathaye, Chynayne and other Oriental Regions'. The British headed that way, as did the Dutchman Willem Barents, who was forced to overwinter on Novaya Zemlya where he and many of his crew died of scurvy. These attempts were stopped by the ice of the Kara Sea, and for a century the area was left to the native Arctic dwellers.

Then, in need of wealth to breathe life into the failing Russian economy, Ivan the Terrible allowed the cossack (from the Chinese word for a man with no king, and later meaning a frontiersman) Ermak to annex Siberia, giving Russia access to its apparently limitless wealth of animal furs. The Russians quickly marched across the vastness of Siberia reaching the Kolyma River by 1642. Then in 1648, in response to rumours of unimaginable riches in sable furs, an expedition was sent out under the protection of the cossack Semen Ivanovich Dezhnev. Encountering favourable ice conditions, Dezhnev rounded what is now called Cape Dezhnev, the Chukchi Peninsula's north-eastern tip, and sighted the Diomede islands. The expedition had passed through the strait that separates Russia and north America, but as the record of the journey was lost for over a century, this piece of water is now called the Bering Strait after a later explorer.

Vitus Bering was a 44-year-old Dane entrusted by Peter the Great to explore east of Chukchi to see if Russia was joined to America. History has been kind to Bering – James Cook, unaware of Dezhnev's journey, named the Strait for him despite Bering never actually having sailed through it. Bering reached St Lawrence Island, but he did not see Alaska and observed only that the local Chukchi coast turned east, not west, before turning south for home. Moscow was not impressed, but strangely was persuaded to give Bering command of a second expedition, on which Europeans landed on Alaska for the first time. Bering and many other members of his crew died of scurvy on one of the Commander Islands, one now called Bering Island in his honour.

Bering's second expedition was a part of what became known as the Great Northern Expedition, an enterprise which surveyed the entire north coast of Russia from the White Sea to Chukchi, and the east coast as far as Japan. This was a monumental exercise, and was completed within a decade. Following the success of the Great Northern Expedition the idea of a North-East Passage was revived. Yet, strangely, it was not a Russian who completed the first transit, but a Swede, Adolf Erik Nordenskiöld, born in Finland of Swedish parents. Nordenskiöld was already an experienced Arctic traveller when in 1878 he acquired the *Vega*, a 300-ton, three-masted whaler with a steam engine. With a crew totalling 30 he sailed from Karlskrona in southern Sweden reaching the Kara Sea in early August. It was ice-free,

left
Vitus Bering. Recently a Danish–Russian expedition located the graves of the men, exhuming Bering's skeleton and recreating his head from the skull. It was discovered that the standard portrait of Bering was not of him at all, but most likely a relative of his mother.

right
Nordenskiöld's ship, the *Vega*, arrived in Stockholm on 24 April 1880 (now known as Vega Day in Sweden) after his epic voyage through the North-East Passage and back to Sweden. Here the ship is anchored below the Royal Palace where King Oscar II gave a reception and dinner for captain and crew.

above
The only photo of Nordenskiöld taken on board the *Vega*.

allowing Nordenskiöld to continue to Cape Chelyuskin where 'the landscape was the dullest and most desolate I have seen in the high north'. By late September, Nordenskiöld estimated he was two days' sailing from Cape Dezhnev, but then ice stopped the ship.

The winter was spent comfortably, the *Vega* being freed from the ice in July 1879. Two days later Nordenskiöld passed Cape Dezhnev and reached the Bering Strait. The completion of the North-East Passage had been a masterpiece of good organisation and seamanship, and is one of the greatest of all polar voyages. But for Nordenskiöld it was merely an hors d'oeuvre, the *Vega* sailing on to Japan, then around China to the Indian Ocean and on to the Suez Canal. She sailed across the Mediterranean, then around Portugal to the English Channel and the North Sea, finally reaching Sweden in April 1880.

left and above
The third transit, and second west–east transit, was made by Roald Amundsen in the *Maud* in 1918–20, an expedition during which two men died as they attempted to reach civilisation after leaving the ship. The reasons why the pair left seem straightforward, but are still debated, adding another controversy to Amundsen's story. Following the expedition, *Maud* was sold to the Hudson's Bay Company. Renamed *Baymaud* she was used as an Arctic supply vessel until she sank in Cambridge Bay. There, her rotting spars can still be seen.

below left
The *Chelyuskin* incident. In the foreground, survivors from the ship erect the camp in which they lived for two months before being rescued by air. In the background the ship's angle suggests that the shot was taken not long before she sank.

After the disastrous defeat in the Russo–Japanese War of 1904–05, the Russian government realised the advantages of a Northern Sea Route, as they called the North-East Passage, and built two ice breakers to explore its possibilities. In these, an expedition under the command of Boris Andreyevich Vilkitskiy, starting from Vladivostok in 1914, completed the second transit of the passage, and the first east–west transit, by reaching Archangel in 1915.

In July 1932 the sealer *Aleksandr Sibiryakov* completed the first transit (going west–east) in a single season, this encouraging the Soviet authorities to send a fleet of 11 ships eastwards in 1933. One was the 4,000 ton *Chelyuskin*, not an ice-breaker, but sufficiently large to nose through significant ice. Entering a narrow lead off Chukchi, the *Chelyuskin* became ice-bound, drifting into Bering Strait, then north-west towards Wrangel Island. After wintering in the ice, on 13 February 1934 the ship was crushed and sank. The 104 survivors set up a camp on the ice from which they were rescued by planes which landed on a runway carved from the sea ice. Following the loss of the *Chelyuskin* there were further transits of the passage in the 1930s, but it has never become a regular route either for Soviet/Russian or other shipping. The passage has also had commercial tourist transits, though these too have been limited in number. Even if global warming should reduce the ice cover north of Siberia, it is likely that Russian nervousness about foreign vessels venturing near its northern shore will mean that transits will never become frequent.

above
Stalin was so delighted by the show of Soviet abilities during the rescue of the *Chelyuskin* survivors that the seven pilots involved were the first to receive the award of Hero of the Soviet Union. Anatoli Lyapidevski, who made the first flight, was the first recipient. Here Stalin is presented with a memento of the rescue.

CANADA

Although the search for the North-West Passage had mapped the coastline of north America and discovered many of Canada's Arctic islands, there was still a vast uncharted area north of the transit line.

In 1902 Otto Sverdrup, captain of the *Fram* on Nansen's expedition, led his own expedition, also in *Fram*, exploring Ellesmere Island's west coast and discovering Axel Heiberg and the Ringnes Islands. Norway's early claim for sovereignty over the islands awakened Canada's latent interest and led to a series of national expeditions to the far north. The early trips were under the command of the Quebecois Joseph-Elzéar Bernier, but in 1913 the Canadian government gave command of an expedition to Vilhjalmur Stefansson, Canadian-born, but of Icelandic parents.

Stefansson's ship was the *Karluk*, its journey becoming an Arctic contemporary of Shackleton's *Endurance*. The ship followed the same pattern – beset in the ice and sinking, the crew facing a difficult journey to land. But there was to be no joyful ending, the *Karluk* crew's retreat being a harrowing tale of death and misery. Nor was their journey behind the guiding light of a great leader, the tale – largely ignored for decades, but recently revived – adding another chapter to the story of a controversial explorer.

The *Karluk* was captained by Bob Bartlett, then considered by many the finest ice captain on the planet. Bartlett had serious reservations about the ship and also about the lack of organisation of the expedition, but nevertheless took *Karluk* northwards in June 1913, heading for Herschel Island, the expedition's winter base. But *Karluk*'s lack of speed meant that when winter came the ship was some way off Herschel and trapped in unrelenting ice. At this point Stefansson announced that he was heading for the shore to hunt caribou and would be gone 10 days. He did not return, but reached Herschel Island from where he sent a message to Ottawa that the ship was entombed in ice and might, or might not,

below
William Laird McKinlay, a young Scot who survived the *Karluk* disaster, cleans his mug before enjoying a meal of blood soup on Wrangel Island. On Wrangel the survivors ate birds' eggs, any plant life they could find and the occasional very welcome seal.

sink. Those on board, he said, would probably survive. Stefansson then headed north to find a continent he was sure lay in the Arctic Ocean.

The *Karluk* and its 25 passengers and crew drifted west to the Bering Strait, then on towards Siberia. On 10 January 1914 the ice finally ruptured the hull. Bartlett now took his crew south towards Wrangel. Four men disappeared on the march, their remains being found years later on the desolate Herald Island. The rest reached Wrangel, but the security the island offered was illusory – Wrangel was uninhabited and animals for food were sparse. Taking one companion, Bartlett therefore crossed the thinning ice sheet to Siberia where he found a village. After resting and eating, Bartlett travelled 650 km (400 miles) to the shore of the Bering Strait and found a ship bound for Alaska.

On Wrangel the situation was now desperate: one frostbitten man needed amputations to stop gangrene, these being carried out by penknife and hacksaw blade. Another man died of a gunshot wound to the head: whether murder or suicide has never been established. Two more died of

starvation, cold and exhaustion. Those remaining were finally rescued by a ship alerted by Bartlett. While war raged in Europe nothing was heard of Stefansson and it was assumed that he, too, had died. Then in 1918, after five years out of contact, he returned. He had found the last three islands of Canada's Arctic archipelago but had not discovered the continent he craved. Despite his abandonment of his expedition and the hideous outcome for those left on the *Karluk*, Stefansson's remarkable survival meant he died a hero while the real hero, Bob Bartlett, was for many years largely ignored.

GREENLAND

In the early 18th century, Denmark sent Hans Egede, a young pastor, to Greenland to look for surviving remnants of the Viking settlers. Egede found no trace, but the visit cemented the Danish claim to the country, one which they have maintained, though Greenland now has home rule.

Greenland's southern coast had been explored by whalers, but the ice-blocked seas of the north and the interior of the country were still unknown. Nordenskiöld, discoverer of the North-East Passage, was one of the first to head inland, certain that the vast inland ice cap was merely a coastal ring hiding a forested centre. His team penetrated about 200 km (125 miles) in 1883 but saw no trace of this assumed forest.

The next to try, in 1886, was Robert Peary, an ambitious American whose name was soon to become synonymous with attempts to reach the North Pole. Peary did not get as far as Nordenskiöld did, but believed that his attempt gave him proprietorial rights over the inland ice and was furious when a young Norwegian, Fridtjof Nansen, crossed Greenland, proving that the interior was an enormous ice cap.

Nansen, who was later to become a distinguished diplomat and winner of the Nobel Peace Prize, started from the east side of Greenland, the opposite side from which Nordenskiöld and Peary had tried. He later claimed that as the east side was largely uninhabited and therefore offered little hope of retreat, this ensured that his team would press on at all costs – death or the west coast, as he put it. More likely is the fact that the west coast had a number of established settlements, which gave him more options in

above

Armed with the single stick then used for cross-country skiing (double sticks not becoming popular until a few years later) the young Fridtjof Nansen was the very image of a Viking. He was popular with ladies (Nansen was having an affair with Scott's wife as her husband was dying in Antarctica), but less so with his team-mates who found him arrogant and overbearing.

Robert Peary learnt well from his Inuit guides, using their clothing and travelling with dogs. But his treatment of the Inuit was very bad, suggesting that he thought he owned them as he did other pieces of useful equipment. This attitude contributed to Cook's antipathy to him and may have led to Cook's claim to the North Pole as a way of paying Peary back.

terms of route: had Nordenskiöld or Peary actually reached the east coast, they would have had to turn around and return, something which Nansen was able to avoid. Nansen's team of five (six with himself) included Otto Sverdrup, and a man who later confessed he had only agreed to go because he was drunk at the time. On the ice cap they manhauled sledges, using primitive sails to help with the work. The west coast (close to Nuuk, Greenland's capital) was reached, after 40 days on the ice.

Peary responded to Nansen's journey by accusing the Norwegian of cheating, and then making his own crossing, west to east, in the unexplored far north of the country. One member of Peary's small team was Dr Frederick Cook, a man who was later to become Peary's bitter rival in the race for the North Pole. Using dog teams, and sending part of the team back early in the

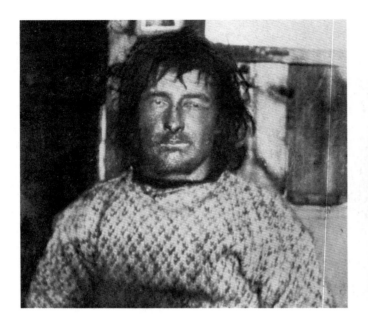

trek to maximise the supplies for those continuing – a technique the British later employed in the
Antarctic – Peary made a remarkable crossing of Greenland. Unfortunately his mis-observation of the
form of the west coast (believing he saw a waterway, the Peary Channel) was later to prove fatal to a
Danish expedition. Peary made several more trips to north-west Greenland, adding to the understanding
of the area's geography, but increasingly his lust for fame drew him into attempts to reach the Pole,
leaving the Danes to fill in the last blank sections of Greenland's coastal map.

The first Danish expedition, seduced by Peary's insistence that a waterway split the northern island,
ended in disaster, three men dying as they attempted to retreat from mapping the true shape of north-east
Greenland. A second expedition was sent, a body from the first trip being buried at the expense of one
man sustaining frostbitten toes which had to be amputated using only a bottle of whisky as anaesthetic.
Then two men, Ejnar Mikkelsen and Iver Iversen, went north alone to find the other bodies. What they did
not know was that during their absence the expedition ship, the *Alabama*, sank. Mikkelsen and Iversen
failed to find the bodies of their countrymen, but did find a note detailing the geography of the north-
east and the fact that the Peary Channel did not exist. The two men then started south, soon experiencing
the same appalling conditions of wet snow that had slowed, then killed the previous team. On the verge
of starvation the pair eventually reached their start point, only to discover the ship sunk and their team
mates gone. Forced to overwinter, the two survived by hunting but the hoped-for rescue failed to materialise
the next summer and they were forced to overwinter again. Only the following summer were they rescued.

Today, in keeping with its status as the largest northern-hemisphere wilderness, Greenland attracts
many expeditions each year, the crossing of its ice cap having become a virtual rite of passage for young
explorers. Yet despite the fact that crossings of the inland ice have become run of the mill, the sheer
size of the island has allowed modern explorers scope for astonishing feats. In 1978 the Japanese Naomi
Uemura used a dog sledge to traverse the ice cap along its 'long axis', the first such traverse, achieved
solo and after first making a solo journey to the North Pole. Then in 1996 two Norwegians, Rune Gjeldnes

above
On the Greenland ice cap
during the epic
south–north traverse of
Rune Gjeldnes and Torry
Larsen. The beautiful
weather belies the epic
qualities of the trip.

below
The Pomores, natives of Russia's north-western Arctic
shore, were famous for their sea voyages. It is conjectured
that they may have made early journeys to Russia's Arctic
islands, and also to Svalbard. This Russian cross on
Kvitøya shows that Russians certainly visited Svalbard,
though the date of such journeys is still debated.

and Torry Larsen, parachuted on to the southern inland ice on 19 March, determined to make the first complete north–south traverse of Greenland. Abseiling down the ice front, they used kayaks in an attempt to paddle to, and around, Kapp Farvel (Cape Farewell), Greenland's southernmost point. This attempt was defeated by weather which made the crossing dangerous, though the two did come within sight of the cape. Having paddled back to the mainland they regained the ice cap and using sails to aid the towing of 175-kg sleds they skied north reaching Cape Morris Jesup where they were collected by air. Their trek of 2,930 km (1,830 miles) was the longest unsupported ski journey at that time, but has lately been bettered by others in Antarctica.

RUSSIA

In 1745 a silk map was sewn for the Czar showing the results of the Great Northern War. It delineated the northern coast of mainland Russia but showed only one archipelago, Novaya Zemlya, of the four that lie off Russia's Arctic coast. A few years later a second island group, the New Siberian Islands, was discovered after a hunter noticed a group of reindeer walking towards him from off the sea ice. Reasoning the animals must be coming from land he followed their tracks north, discovering an island on which he found clear signs that other hunters had preceded him, but remained silent so that they could exploit the islands in peace.

The most northerly island group, Franz Josef Land, was found in 1873 by an Austro–Hungarian expedition. This expedition, aboard the *Tegetthof*, was attempting, in the face of all known facts, to sail north over the Pole to China. Becoming trapped in the ice the crew were forced to overwinter, carried north by the drifting ice. One day, when fog which had shrouded them for days lifted, the men were amazed to see land which they named for their Emperor. When the hoped-for release of the ship did not materialise the men abandoned her and marched south across the pack ice. After many weeks of arduous travel they resighted the ship, realising that days of hard effort had been wiped out by the drift of the

ice. Desperate, but realising that to regain the ship was futile, they set out again, this time reaching Novaya Zemlya where, on the brink of starvation, they were rescued by a Russian ship.

The final archipelago, Severnaya Zemlya, was not found until the early years of the 20th century, with the expeditions of Vilkitskiy which culminated in the first east–west transit of the North-East Passage. Vilkitskiy used two ice-breakers, each modelled on the world's first ice-breaker, the *Ermak*. Though *Ermak* was Russian in concept and ownership, the ship was actually built in Newcastle-upon-Tyne, England in 1898. *Ermak* was the brainchild of Vice-Admiral Markov of the Russian navy and was used in an attempt to reach the North Pole in 1899, which failed at 81°28'N. That attempt, and the later enthusiasm for transits of the North-East Passage, led to an expedition which has only recently received the interest it deserves.

The *Saint Anna* left Murmansk in September 1914, far too late in the year for an attempt on the passage, the decision indicating the lack of experience of the ship's captain, Georgi Brusilov. Soon the ship was ice-bound, and after two winters, had drifted towards the northern tip of Franz Josef Land. At that point relations between Brusilov and his deputy Valerian Albanov broke down, and Albanov decided to leave the ship and walk south. Together with 13 men who feared the ship was doomed, Albanov set out on the 120 km (74 miles) walk to Franz Josef. After 11 days of exhausting effort the men had walked just 5 km (3 miles) south, but drifted 22 km (13 miles) north: three men then abandoned the attempt and returned to the ship. The rest continued, shooting seals for food and fuel (heating water by burning blubber)

below

Though *Ermak* was Russian in concept and ownership, the ship was actually built in Newcastle-upon-Tyne, England in 1898/9.

and using kayaks when they reached occasional stretches of open water. After 10 weeks they reached Franz Josef. By now, men were dying of exhaustion, but Albanov kept them marching, finding a note left by Frederick Jackson that finally fixed his position. The survivors now split into groups. Some used kayaks while others skied, Albanov and another man being split off from their group of kayakers and almost killed by a violent storm. Eventually Albanov and his companion Konrad reached Cape Flora where they found another Russian expedition. Of their comrades nothing was ever seen again. The *Saint Anna* and the remaining crew also disappeared without trace.

TO THE POLE

The first genuine attempt on the Pole was made in 1773 by Englishman Constantine Phipps whose crew included a 14-year-old midshipman called Horatio Nelson who narrowly avoided being killed by a polar bear. Phipps was followed by Parry, hero of the North-West Passage. Parry's attempt to manhaul sledges on which rested the ship's boats (in case open water was found) was doomed by the

THE WALLSEND SLIPWAY
AND
ENGINEERING Cº LTD
ENGINES Nº 491
1899.
NEWCASTLE ON TYNE

sheer effort required: occasionally his team made only 250 m (820 ft) of headway in an hour of hard pulling. In 1872, Parry reached 82°45′N, a record at the time.

The next attempts were American. Elisha Kent Kane headed north in 1855, his surgeon on that trip, Isaac Hayes, trying again in 1860. But these were primarily Franklin search expeditions, the first genuine American trip being in 1871 when Charles Francis Hall sailed the *Polaris* north between Ellesmere Island and Greenland. The attempt ended in tragedy, Hall dying and being buried on Greenland's shore, and the expedition breaking up in confusion. Some team members were left on an ice floe when the ship was unexpectedly driven away by a gale, though both these men and those on the ship survived.

Following Hall's attempt the British tried once more, George Nares sailing two ships to Ellesmere's northern shore, one of the most remarkable feats of seamanship in polar history. From the winter camp Lieutenant Albert Markham took a sledge party north, establishing a new northing record of 83°20′26″N on 12 May 1876. Despite the brilliance of Nares' seamanship, the new record and the considerable exploration undertaken, the expedition almost ended in disaster, 80 per cent of the men contracting scurvy. Years before, John Rae had realised that fresh meat, fish and vegetables were effective anti-scorbutants, and it was well known that lime juice aged badly and so became less effective with time. But a committee set up to investigate the shortcomings of the Nares trip concluded that nothing could have been

below left
During the attempt to resupply Greely's expedition, the *Proteus* was trapped in the ice and sank. The ship had been under the command of Ernest Garlington, an odd choice as he was a cavalry officer, promoted when many of the officers on his unit, the 7th Cavalry, were killed with Custer at the Little Big Horn. Garlington later won the Congressional Medal of Honor for his part in the infamous attack on the Indians at Wounded Knee.

below
Suspicion over Hall's death existed from the day it was reported, but was confirmed by an exhumation and autopsy carried out in 1968, which showed that Hall had died of arsenic poisoning. Whether this was self-administered during a bout of prolonged ill-health, or whether it was murder, cannot now be established. Many favour the latter, but the name and motive of any guilty party remains elusive.

right
Greely's tent,
photographed by the
expedition's rescuers.
Evidence of cannibalism
found at the camp was
hushed up in the official
enquiry which tactfully
decided that any flesh
which had been
removed from dead
bodies had been taken
'with a view no doubt to
use as shrimp bait'.

improved, either on the matter of anti-scorbutants or equipment. One of the committee was a cousin of Albert Markham: Clements Markham was later instrumental in appointing Robert Falcon Scott to lead the expeditions to Antarctica.

The Americans were back in 1881, Adolphus Washington Greely taking the *Proteus* north to Nares, winter camp and establishing a base – Fort Conger – there. The *Proteus* then sailed south again. Greely's trip had a dual purpose: he intended to reach the Pole but was also carrying out scientific studies. The first objective failed, though James Lockwood led a team which passed Markham's record by 6.5 km (4 miles).

The second objective was achieved, Ellesmere Island being explored, but things then began to go wrong. The expected relief ship failed to appear and, with food running low and another winter approaching, Greely decided to abandon Fort Conger, taking his expedition south to Cape Sabine where the relief ship was supposed to have dropped supplies if it could not reach Fort Conger. Reaching the Cape, Greely found no supplies – it was going to be a long, hungry winter. A relief expedition had been sent, the *Proteus* again, but had become entombed in ice and sank. Though the crew survived, back in the US the Secretary of War, Robert Lincoln, son of Abraham, vetoed a further attempt to go north. Greely had been abandoned.

On Pym Island near Cape Sabine, Greely's men built a rough hut of stone around an upturned boat. The area was devoid of animals and as winter approached the men were forced on to starvation rations. Soup was made by boiling rope and boot soles, then the buffalo hide sleeping bags which were the men's only protection against the cold. One man caught stealing food was court-martialled, sentenced to death and shot. The expedition doctor died the same day, probably a suicide by self-administered drugs. By spring the few men left alive were eating candles, what was left of old leather strips, seaweed and anything else they could find. But now, back in Washington the consciences of the nation's governors were finally pricked and a rescue was organised. It found just seven of 25 men alive. One of the rescued men died soon after: the frostbite of his hands and feet was so bad that bones stuck out from the rotting flesh and even amputation could not save him.

Two years before Greely set out, another American expedition had headed north. Led by George

Washington De Long in the *Jeanette*, it was intended to discover if Wrangel Island was part of a continent that reached as far as Greenland. De Long also hoped he would find an open polar sea and so be able to reach the North Pole. The *Jeanette* sailed in July 1879, reaching pack ice close to Herald Island where she was soon beset. De Long hoped he might now drift north to open water, but instead he went north-west, passing close enough to Wrangel to realise it was a small island rather than part of a larger land mass. For two years the *Jeanette* drifted, but was then crushed by the ice, the crew abandoning her just before she sank.

The crew headed south hauling the three ship's boats. It took 47 days to reach Bennett, the most northerly of the New Siberian Islands, and after a ten-day rest the men set out for mainland Russia. They were now rowing their boats, picking a route through the drifting pack ice. Though De Long was anxious to keep the boats together, a storm blew up separating the three: no trace of the smallest boat or its crew of eight was ever found. The other two boats reached the coast near the Lena Delta. One of them was lucky enough to be discovered by local Tungus who provided food and shelter, but De Long's boat, with 13 men aboard, landed in the maze of streams of the delta. Forced to wade ashore through new-forming ice to reach marshy ground, the men were chilled and exhausted and soon started to die of cold. The survivors struggled inland in the hope of finding a village, but with many of the men too weak to continue De Long decided to send the two strongest men ahead while he remained with the others. The two met their colleagues from the second boat, but by the time they had returned to De Long, he and all the other men were dead. In all 20 men had died, with little to show for the loss except the discovery of two small islands. Yet the *Jeanette* tragedy was to be the basis of the most audacious of all Arctic journeys.

Two years after De Long's body was found, the 23-year-old Fridtjof Nansen read an article about relics of the *Jeanette* being found on an ice floe off the south-west coast of Greenland. The author of the article conjectured that the discovery implied a current flowing across the Arctic Ocean, and Nansen realised that such a current might take a ship over, or very close to, the North Pole. If the ship could survive being trapped in the ice it would be released near the coast of Greenland.

When it sailed, *Fram* had a crew of 13 including Nansen, and was skippered by Otto Sverdrup, veteran of the Greenland crossing. The ship sailed through the Kara Sea, around Cape Chelyuskin and then north to enter the pack. On 5 October 1893 the rudder was raised: *Fram* was frozen in. At first, to Nansen's confusion, the ship drifted south, but soon began the expected steady drift north. After drifting through two Arctic winters it became clear that the ship was

above

The older Nansen. After the *Fram* expedition Nansen became the guru of polar travel but did not make another significant trip. In old age he became a distinguished diplomat and was awarded the Nobel Peace Prize for his work to relieve the suffering of Russian famine victims.

going to miss the Pole and Nansen decided to set out with one companion, Hjalmar Johansen, to try to reach it by sledge. By the time the pair left, *Fram* was at 83°50'N and had broken Lockwood's northing record: the ship was also still heading north.

Nansen and Johansen took three sledges, more than 20 dogs and 760 kgs (1675 lbs) of equipment. The pair thought the journey would be easy, but the pressure ridges in the sea ice and dreadful cold slowed progress so that after 24 days, at 86°14'N, a new record, they realised that the Pole was out of reach, and turned south. Any chance of regaining the ship seemed futile and so the pair headed for Franz Josef Land. The two men made better speed heading south but soon had a crisis when they forgot to wind their watches. Without them they could not be sure of their longitude and so could not be certain where Franz Josef was. That, and the toll taken by the routine duty of killing dogs for food, began to wear them down. As the days dragged past, unable to kill the last of the dogs, as they could not manage to haul the sledges themselves, both men and dogs began to starve. Then, after 100 days away from the *Fram*, Johansen shot a seal, the first of several, and things started to improve.

The sea ice was now also interspersed with large stretches of open water, allowing the pair to kayak rather than sledge which made progress easier. Finally they sighted land, discovering later that they were in north-eastern Franz Josef. Forced to overwinter on Franz Josef the men survived on a diet of walrus and polar bear meat. When summer came they kayaked south and by great good fortune arrived on the island on which the English explorer Frederick Jackson had set up his base. Alerted by the barking of dogs the two men skied to the camp where they were greeted by Jackson, who recognised the dirty, long-haired Nansen.

Nansen returned to Oslo a hero, and history has, in general, agreed with this assessment, but there were some who, from the first, thought otherwise, believing that for a leader to abandon his expedition could never be justified, that the trek had been foolhardy and that Nansen should have tried to return to *Fram*. Peary, still smarting over the Greenland crossing 'cheat', wondered why Nansen had not returned to *Fram* – 'he could certainly have followed his own trail back ... (the ship) would drift very little in five or six weeks ... was he ashamed to go back after so short an absence?'

As the Norwegians were returning from Franz Josef Land explorers from neighbouring Sweden were preparing to try to reach the Pole using new technology, a balloon. Salomon Andrée had been interested in balloons for many years, but not until 1894 did he consider the idea of using one to reach the Pole. A first attempt in 1896 failed even before take-off, but in 1897 Andrée was back. With Nils Strindberg and Knut Frænkel he took off in the *Örnen* (*Eagle*) from Virgo Harbour on Spitsbergen. In one sense Andrée's idea was well considered: the balloon was adequately leak-proof and earlier flights in Sweden had shown that at low altitudes trailing ropes offered limited steering. But there were also glaring flaws in the planning. Even if the Pole was reached there was little chance of touching down and little account had been taken of the effect of ice on the fabric – Andrée just hoped that if he flew low enough ice would not form. On take-off the trailing ropes were lost, the *Eagle* rising rapidly to 600 m (1,968 ft); Andrée had lost both his steering and his 'protection' against icing. The balloon headed north-east and an hour later disappeared from view.

In those pre-radio days Andrée had taken buoys and carrier pigeons to keep in touch. The buoys were found, eventually, as was a single pigeon (it was shot before having had a chance to fly home), but they were the last messages from the team. Then, 33 years later, Norwegian scientists landed at Kvitøya. The men found a snow-covered camp and the remains of the three balloonists. Later searches revealed diaries and, most remarkable of all, a camera with film intact and still capable of development. It revealed a series of poignant shots of the last moments of the flight and the subsequent camp. Rain had caused the balloon to lose height and eventually the gondola hit the ice. It had travelled 830 km (515 miles) in 65½ hours. The three men headed south hauling three sledges, reaching Kvitøya on 5 October with an overwintering inevitable. The diary entries stopped a few weeks later.

Strindberg had clearly died first as his body was buried beneath rocks, though his death must have

below
A photograph by Nils Strindberg of the *Eagle* soon after it had landed on the ice. This was one of a series of photographs developed when the Andrée team's camera was discovered.

opposite

Andrée's campsite on
Kvitøya, a rarely visited
island in north-eastern
Svalbard.

above

Just before the launch of the *Eagle*. The exposed and
downright precarious nature of the venture is obvious
from the open gondola and limited equipment. Despite
the doomed nature of the flight, it is hard not feel
sympathy with the men who were brave almost beyond
belief. The aftermath of the discovery of the bodies of the
three was as poignant as the can be imagined.
Strindberg's young fiancée, eventually giving up hope of
his safe return, married an Englishman and settled in
America where she gave piano lessons, one of the
expedition's stuffed pigeons hanging above the
instrument. She died before the bodies were discovered,
but her husband did not. On hearing of the discovery, he
had her body exhumed and sent her heart to Sweden to
be buried beside her first love.

occurred after the last entries in the diaries of Andrée and Frœnkel as there is no mention of it in them.
The cause of death of all three has been subject of speculation ever since the discovery. From the photos
and diaries it is clear that polar bears were shot for food. Analysis of meat samples discovered at the
camp showed the presence of *trichinae* (a parasitic nematode). If the meat had been eaten raw or poorly
cooked, the men could have developed trichinosis and died of it. That is still the opinion of many experts,
though cold, exhaustion and even suicide induced by their hopeless position cannot be ruled out.

The next attempt on the Pole was by an Italian team led by the Duke of the Abruzzi, who was later to
lead the first attempt to climb K2, the world's second-highest mountain. The Italians, heading north in
1899, chose Franz Josef Land as their starting point, Umberto Cagni leading three others on a 104-day trek
across 1,200 km of sea ice to reach 86°34′N, a new northing record. On his return, Cagni claimed that
the journey over the sea-ice was too difficult and that future attempts should be made from Greenland.
His advice was ignored by the American William Ziegler who financed two attempts from Franz Josef,
each of which failed miserably. Neither, probably, did Cagni's advice influence the efforts of Robert Peary,
the next American to try, Peary's experience in Greenland persuading him that he had already found the
correct jumping-off point.

Peary first tried in 1902, reaching 84°17′N, but it was a curiously tentative attempt, one that so
bothered his backers that they asked Frederick Cook to examine him to see if he was still capable of
leading such trips. The meeting between the two further soured a relationship which was already strained
in the wake of their shared Greenland expedition. Cook's view was that the 46-year-old Peary, who had
lost toes to frostbite during a previous Greenland expedition was finished as an Arctic traveller.

Yet Peary found backers for a new trip and in 1905 he went north again. After overwintering near Nares'
base, Peary went north with dog sledges, claiming a new northing record of 87°6′N on 21 April 1906. It is
a record which many find dubious, requiring remarkable speed over the last few days from a man troubled
by amputated toe stubs and a hernia. Expert opinion favours Peary falling just short of Cagni's record.

No further records were claimed for three years. Then, in September 1909, an astonished world was
informed that the North Pole had finally been reached, not once, but twice. On 2 September Frederick
Cook announced that he had stood at the Pole on 21 April 1908. On 6 September Robert Peary stated
that he had reached the Pole on 6 April 1909. A thorough examination of the claims of Cook and Peary is
beyond the scope of this book. Indeed, whole books have been written on the topic, each still having
supporters willing to defy logic and good manners in support of their man. Cook claims to have reached
the Pole with two Inuit companions, Ahwelah and Etukishook, two sledges and 26 dogs from the northern
tip of Axel Heiberg Island. Peary is known to have set out from northern Ellesmere Island with 24 men,
19 sledges and 133 dogs, sending groups of men back after camps had been established. Finally he sent
his last support team, led by Bob Bartlett, later the captain of the *Karluk*, back (from 87°46′49″N)
continuing with his African American 'manservant' Matthew Henson, four Inuit, six sledges and 40 dogs.

Against Cook's claim is the fact that his Inuit companions were later to say that they had never been
out of sight of land (a fact which weighed heavily after Cook's claim to have climbed Mount McKinley
was 'exposed' as a fraud by his companion: in each case these counterclaims are themselves subject to
dispute), that his return route made claims on the geography of the Ringnes Islands which were false

and that he did not mention seeing a previously unknown island he would have had to pass. Against Peary's claim is the phenomenal speed he claimed for his last dash to the Pole, a speed which has never been repeated. Against both men is the fact that they had critical failings as navigators. Cook was poor in calculating both latitude and longitude; Peary was good on latitude, but made no attempt to establish his longitude, claiming he used dead reckoning, a near impossibility on shifting ice and where straight lines cannot be travelled.

In the aftermath of the claims, Peary's supporters were the harder hitters and Cook was discredited. But Cook never admitted to fraud. Whatever the truth of his claim, his actual journey was by far the most interesting. Today Peary is credited with being first by all except the experts in the field, most of whom consider his case fraudulent. Once Peary's claim had been accepted explorers lost interest in sea-ice journeys to the Pole. But attempts by air became fashionable as balloons and planes became more capable and reliable in the aftermath of the 1914–18 war.

The following year Amundsen and Ellsworth were back at King's Bay ready to try for the Pole again, but this time in an airship, a dirigible which was designed by the Italian Umberto Nobile. While waiting for good weather another American, Richard Byrd, arrived with his Fokker tri-motor named the *Josephine Ford*, and pilot Floyd Bennett. This pair took off before the

left
Cook's igloo camp at the North Pole. His Inuit companions later said that at no point had they been out of sight of land, making a pole trip impossible. However, they had come under extreme pressure to change their story and, as Peary's supporters knew, were usually willing to say what their employers wanted to hear.

above
Inuit from Peary's expedition at the North Pole, a hand-tinted photograph. Suspicion over whether Peary made it to the Pole has grown ever since his trip.

In 1925 Roald Amundsen teamed up with the American Lincoln Ellsworth, the two buying a pair of Dornier-Wal planes which flew north from Ny Ålesund on Spitsbergen in 1925. Each plane carried three men and food for three weeks, the plan being to land at the Pole, transferring all fuel and men into one plane for a continuing flight to Alaska. After eight hours the planes landed, but sightings showed they were only at 88°N. The return was epic, a runway having to be stamped out of the ice – a process which took weeks – and take-off missing an iceberg by a whisker.

airship, returning after 16 hours claiming to have reached the Pole.

Of Amundsen's airship flight there are no doubts. On 11 May 1926, the *Norge* lifted off from Ny Ålesund with a crew of 16 (including Amundsen, Ellsworth, Nobile and Oscar Wisting who had been with Amundsen to the South Pole). At 1.30am on 12 May the airship circled over the pole. Amundsen and Wisting, the first two men to see both poles (and, probably, in the teams that were first to reach each) shook hands. The *Norge* then flew on to Teller, Alaska.

So infatuated with his perceived success did Nobile become that, in 1928, he ran his own expedition in a new airship called *Italia*. It was a disaster, the airship icing heavily and crashing. Six men were hauled off to their doom by the freed balloon, one more died on the ice and several others were badly injured. Nobile sustained a broken arm and leg. The Italian support ship bungled the rescue, sending out press statements instead of listening for radio messages and eventually three of the nine survivors set off to reach help. Finally a radio amateur in Arkhangelsk heard the survivor's SOS and informed Moscow.

right
Amundsen (left), and Ellsworth (right), congratulate Byrd and Bennett. In 1960 – after both Bennett and Byrd had died – it was proved by an analysis of aircraft and wind speed data that their claim was false. Bennett is also said to have confided in a friend before his premature death from cancer that the flight was a fraud, the *Josephine Ford* developing a fault which precluded an attempt soon after take off, the pair merely flying around Spitsbergen until it was time to return.

A full-scale rescue involving 18 ships, 22 planes and 1,500 men of six nations was now put into operation. A plane located the crash site and landed, returning with Nobile and his pet dog. The watching world was appalled and despite Nobile's protestations that he accepted being the first to be rescued in order to co-ordinate further recovery efforts, a furious Mussolini demoted him for making Italy a laughing stock. On the next flight the rescue plane crashed, adding the pilot to the list of those trapped. It took a further 18 days before the Russian ice-breaker *Krassin* was able to rescue the other survivors (and the hapless pilot). The *Krassin* also picked up two of the three men who attempted to go for help and, adding to the horror of it all, one of these seemed sleekly healthy, a strange contrast to the other survivor whose condition was so poor he later died. The healthy man admitted eating the third, missing, companion, though this story was hushed up amid speculation that murder might have preceded cannibalism.

above
Umberto Nobile in the *Norge* during the North Pole flight.

above right
Amundsen (left), and Ellsworth (right), either side of Mussolini. The *Norge* flight had been a success, but the aftermath was ugly despite this photo of smiling faces. Nobile tried to claim all the credit for the trip, aided by Mussolini who basked in the Italian's reflected glory.

To add one last dreadful strand to the tale, the *Italia* disaster also resulted in Amundsen's death. Hearing of Nobile's predicament he immediately offered his services, claiming past disagreements meant nothing when lives were at stake. Mussolini turned down the great man's help. Amundsen was nearing his fifty-sixth birthday, but looked much older and had become paranoid and bitter in his old age. The rejection made matters worse. Amundsen decided to help despite the refusal and when the French offered him a seaplane for a private mission, he accepted. It was soon clear that the Latham 47 plane was not up to the job, but Amundsen had given his word and so, with six men on board, it took off on 18 June. It was never seen again.

above

Nobile's attempt to prove himself a great explorer with the *Italia* ended in disaster with eight men dead and Amundsen dying in a rescue attempt. The attempt to rescue the survivors of the airship almost ended in tragedy when the Swede Einar Lundborg, having brought out Nobile on his first flight, crashed on his second and was lucky to escape serious injury. The crash meant that in an instant Lundborg had to be reclassified from potential rescuer to survivor.

above right

The last photo of Roald Amundsen. Ten weeks after his plane went missing a fisherman hauled in a float and fuel tank from the plane. It seemed they had been removed in an attempt to construct a raft, a poignant reminder that Amundsen, if it was indeed he that organised the construction, never gave up on a project, and had only ever failed this once.

right

Papanin's tent on the ice. His team had landed 25 km (17 miles) from the pole and drifted until February 1938 when they were rescued from a melting floe near east Greenland.

In the Soviet Union after the successful outcome of the *Chelyuskin* ice camp, the authorities decided on a logical extension, the deliberate use of a floe camp ice drift allowing science to be pursued across the Arctic Ocean. The first such drift station was set up in June 1937, with four men under Ivan Papanin. The 1939–45 war ended a projected Soviet drift station programme, but it began again in 1950, a series of stations being set up and manned through to the 1980s. As a prelude to the 1950 stations the Soviets also landed an aircraft at the Pole on 23 April 1948, the team of scientists – Somov, Sen'ko, Ostrekin and Gordienko – becoming the first men confirmed to have stood there. Ten years later, on 4 August 1958, the US Navy submarine USS *Nautilus*, commanded by W. R. Anderson, reached the Pole on a sub-surface crossing of the Arctic Ocean. Eight days later the USS *Skate*, surfaced at the pole. Not until 1977 did a surface ship get there, the nuclear-powered Russian ice-breaker *Arktika* arriving on 18 August.

It was not until 1968 – 50 years after the first claim – that men reached the pole again (or for the first time, if earlier claims are discounted) over the ice, a Canadian/US team led by Ralph Plaisted using snowmobiles to travel from Ward Hunt Island, off Ellesmere Island's northern coast. The same year a team of four set out to cross the Arctic by way of the Pole. The British TransArctic Expedition led by Wally Herbert set out from Barrow on Alaska's north coast on 21 February 1963 with 40 dogs and four sledges. Sustained by air drops and spending winter on the ice, the team reached Svalbard the following April after a journey of 407 days.

above

A self-portrait during
Børge Ousland's
unsupported North Pole
trek. Ousland later
repeated the feat during
a solo crossing of the
Arctic Ocean.

Later trips to the Pole filled in the perceived gaps in human endeavour. In 1978 the Japanese Naomi Uemura reached the Pole solo with a dog sledge, then in 1986 Frenchman Jean-Louis Etienne made a solo ski journey, with air resupply every 10 days. The first unsupported journey was made in 1986 when a team of eight, led by Will Steger and Paul Schurke, used dog teams hauling 3 tons of equipment. In 1990 the Norwegians Erling Kagge and Børge Ousland made an unsupported ski trek from Ward Hunt Island. (They had started as a threesome, but on the ninth day Geir Randby had injured his back and had to be evacuated.) Ousland was back in 1994 making a solo, unsupported trek from Cape Arktichesky at the northern end of Severnaya Zemlya.

The next landmark was the unsupported crossing of the Arctic Ocean in 2000 by the Norwegians Rune Gjeldnes and Torry Larsen, the pair starting from Cape Arktichesky and reaching Ellesmere Island's Cape Discovery after a trek of 109 days. Finally Ousland returned yet again, repeating this trek solo and unsupported in 2001. Purists will argue that Ousland's journey was not totally unsupported as his sledge was replaced and he accepted a meal of chilli con carne at the pole from others he met there, but there is no doubting the magnitude of the achievement. The dangers of sea ice and polar bears will always make the Arctic a more demanding place than Antarctica for the trekker, even if today tourists can buy a passage on an ice-breaker and enjoy a luxury cruise to the Pole.

FIRST SIGHT, FIRST STEP, FIRST WINTER

In 1773 James Cook became the first man to cross the Antarctic Circle, eventually reaching 67°31'S between the Amundsen and Ross Seas, but it was another 50 years before man saw the continent. In 1820 Thaddens von Bellingshausen — the common form of the Russian name — was exploring the Southern Ocean looking for a base for Russia's Pacific fleet. On 27 January 1820 he observed 'a solid stretch of ice running from east to west'. It is very probable that Bellingshausen was seeing the western edge of the Fimbul Ice Shelf, though it is doubtful whether he knew what he was looking at. Some experts doubt whether this was actually the first sighting as by 1820 the islands of the Southern Ocean – South Georgia, the South Shetlands, etc. – had already been visited by sealing boats for over 50 years. The sealers were jealous of their own private beaches and if one or more had actually found rich pickings on the continent the last thing they would have done was broadcast the discovery and so share their find. The glory of finding a new continent is one thing, but money in the bank is quite another.

After the sealers came the whalers. Their endeavours were greatly enhanced and accelerated by the Norwegian Svend Foyn, who designed the first steam-powered whale boat and invented the explosive harpoon, allowing the fast rorquals to be hunted. The effect was the annihilation of the Southern Ocean's whale population.

As well as the commercial ships in southern waters there were also national expeditions whose primary interest was scientific. The Frenchman Jules-Sébastien-César Dumont d'Urville came in 1837 to look for the magnetic South Pole. He failed to find it – but named the Adélie penguin after his wife! The American Charles Wilkes arrived the following year, a tyrannical commander, loathed by his crew. He surveyed about 2,500 km (1,700 miles) of Antarctica's coast, but for so large and expensive an expedition this was seen as a poor reward. Back in France, Dumont d'Urville was fêted, and he and his crews given large rewards. In the US, Wilkes was court-martialled, charged with inaccurate surveying and the harsh treatment of his crew.

The third science-based expedition of the time was led by James Clark Ross, who was already a veteran of several Arctic journeys. In 1840 Ross headed south, reaching 78°9'S, a new record. He was the first to see what is now called the Ross Ice Shelf and also named the two volcanoes on Ross Island, Erebus and Terror, after his two ships. Later the two peaks were to watch over the attempts of the British to reach the South Pole.

Yet despite these expeditions no foot had yet touched the newly discovered continent – unless, of course, the feet of secretive sealers had done so years before. The official first step had to wait until January 1895, though exactly whose foot was to be the subject of arguments which reached the pages of *The Times* of London. The expedition that caused the furore sailed in the *Antarctic*, a Norwegian vessel equipped by Svend Foyn whose harpoon had made him rich. The ship was captained by Leonard Kristensen, the crew including the Norwegian Carsten Borchgrevink, a teacher then resident in Australia. On 24 January the expedition reached Cape Adare. As the ship's boat beached, Kristensen, at the prow, stepped ashore, while Borchgrevink leapt into the water from the stern and rushed forward to beach the craft. At the same time, Alexander Van Tunzelman, a Campbell Island youth who had joined the ship in New Zealand, jumped ashore to hold the boat for his captain. Later, all three claimed to have been first man ashore, the argument never being satisfactorily resolved.

The next major landmark was the first overwintering in Antarctica. That

came in 1898 when the *Belgica* spent the winter entombed in the ice of the Bellingshausen Sea. The ship was owned by a Belgian, Adrian de Gerlache, who was also the leader of the expedition, and included Roald Amundsen, on his first polar journey, and Dr Frederick Cook. The two men got on well. Cook, despite the bad press he was to receive (and still does), was a brilliant polar explorer whose innovative ideas were to influence many, including both Peary and Amundsen, and whose optimism in the face of difficulties was an inspiration. Amundsen, learning from Cook during the *Belgica* trip, was to become the greatest of all polar explorers.

Though taciturn (to be polite) and so apparently very different to the outgoing Cook, Amundsen remained an admirer and visited Cook in prison after he had been wrongly indicted for fraud. This simple, compassionate act brought Amundsen considerable criticism and is a clear indication of the great man's regard for Cook.

It seems likely that de Gerlache had always intended to overwinter in the pack ice but when Cook and Amundsen realised this they were unhappy as there was no hope of rescue if the ship was crushed. Ignoring them de Gerlache headed south. There was a somewhat muted protest, but by the time de Gerlache had been persuaded to head north it was too late: the ship was entombed. The winter seems to have been pleasant enough, though with occasional scares when the drifting ice threatened to hole the ship. The crew stayed healthy, in large part due to Cook's insistence on a fresh meat diet and a 'light' cure, each man being required to spend time near the heat and light of the stove every day. Unfortunately the fresh meat was penguin. One man said he would rather die than eat penguin. It was a prophetic comment: he did not eat it and died of scurvy.

When the sun returned it seemed the ice would never free the ship, and again it was Cook who came up with an idea, suggesting carving a channel towards open water, an idea which the British navy had used to good effect several times in the Arctic. On 15 February 1899 the *Belgica* broke free of the pack which held her, though it was another month before she reached entirely ice-free waters. Two days after she broke free, another ship, the *Southern Cross*, sighted Cape Adare.

The *Southern Cross* was commanded by Carsten Borchgrevink who, having been refused official support for an overwintering trip, had acquired private backing for an expedition that was to be the first to overwinter on the continent. The expedition was largely Norwegian but included an Englishman and a Belgian. There were also two Lapps who had with them a pack of sledge dogs. When the expedition unloaded, the dogs immediately slaughtered the local penguin colony.

The expedition was very well organised, but unfortunately Cape Adare was unsuited to a winter camp. Borchgrevink chose it because he knew he could get ashore there, but had not reckoned with the

violent winds that strafed it, or with the difficulty of reaching the 'true' continent above its rocky cliffs. Despite problems over Borchgrevink's leadership the expedition did rather well, spending a reasonably comfortable winter and doing good work. One man, Nicolai Hanson, a Norwegian zoologist died, probably of scurvy, though he did not exhibit the classic symptoms: he was the first man to die on the continent, and also the first to be buried there.

Back in Britain, Borchgrevink's dispute over Hanson's notes ensured that when the Royal Geographical Society decided to support a national Antarctic expedition, his name was not even in the frame as leader. The dispute also reached the pages of *The Times*, one man embroiled in the argument being Edward Wilson. Sir Clements Markham, the Society's President, noted that Borchgrevink was not a scientist and the leader of such an expedition should be one. Later he appointed Robert Falcon Scott, a naval officer and certainly no scientist. In reality what Markham disliked most about Borchgrevink was that he was not English. In 1899 in a speech in Berlin, Markham ignored the contributions of all non-British explorers and proposed that to aid future exploration the continent should be divided into four quadrants, Weddell, Enderby, Ross and Victoria – three named for British explorers, the fourth for the British Queen. The arrogant assumption that only Britain had the right to explore Antarctica was backed by the equally arrogant proposition that only the British knew how to do it, an assumption that would lead, eventually, but inevitably, to disaster.

TO THE POLE: EARLY ATTEMPTS

When the British National Antarctic Expedition finally started out in 1901 it was led by Scott and included Edward Wilson as naturalist and assistant doctor, and a young Irish merchant marine officer, Ernest Shackleton. Despite Scott having visited Nansen, the guru of polar exploration, his ship, *Discovery*, was built along the lines of those that had failed in the Arctic rather than those of *Fram*. This fitted well with Markham's prejudices, Markham also being against the use of dogs and skis. Markham had been appalled

above

Scott's *Discovery* expedition made the first balloon flights over Antarctica – using a tethered, hydrogen-filled balloon. Scott himself made the first flight, much to the disgust of Wilson who wrote 'knowing nothing whatever about the business, (Scott) insisted on going up first and through no fault of his own came back safely'.

right

Shackleton, Scott and Wilson after the furthest south journey. The return journey had been terrible. The weather broke and, with the last dog killed, the manhauling took a heavy toll of sick men. Shackleton became so ill, Wilson thought he would die. A lesser man probably would have, but Shackleton's ferocious will kept him going. After 93 days on the ice the exhausted trio finally reached the *Discovery*.

that Peary and others had shot dogs to feed not only the remaining dogs, but themselves. To a man raised in the fox-hunting tradition such behaviour was beyond the pale. At the recent funeral of Queen Victoria navy men had manhauled the gun carriage carrying her coffin. It struck him as a beautiful vision, one which could be easily transferred to the Antarctic.

Scott usually followed Markham's advice, but his trip to Nansen – despite it being 'rather wasted time' – had impressed on him the idea that dogs and skis were valuable. Sadly he had only half understood. Failing to learn to control dogs or to ski, his men were hopeless at both and at one stage on the trip Scott's men manhauled a sledge on which they stored their skis, their dogs trotting along beside them.

The expedition overwintered at Hut Point, close to McMurdo Sound; then, in the austral summer of 1902–03, Scott decided to take a team of three, himself, Shackleton and Wilson, south. He hoped to reach the Pole but probably realised that he would be lucky to make it, travel across inland Antarctica never having been attempted before. Because no supply dumps had been laid, the three men made slow progress, constantly having to return to recover supplies that were too heavy to haul in one go. Nevertheless they established a new record southing, passing 82°S. By then both Scott and Shackleton were ill, each showing symptoms of scurvy. Despite their reservations they had been forced to eat dog flesh and Wilson was demoralised at being the one deputed to kill the dogs; and having only a scalpel this was a messy, distressing task. He had wanted to return earlier, but Scott insisted on continuing. There

Shackleton.   Capt. Scott.   Wilson.

On arrival at the ship after 3 months Southern Sledge Journey.
Nov. 2. 02 — Feb. 2. 03.   82°17'S.

was also friction between Scott and Shackleton
(the start of an antithesis which was to mark their
later careers): from the final camp at 82°15′S
Scott and Wilson continued alone to 82°17′S,
Shackleton being ordered to stay behind.

The team spent a second winter at their base,
Scott exploring westwards the following year
before sailing the *Discovery* north for home.
Overall it had been a successful trip and Scott
returned a hero. His book on the expedition was a
best-seller, but it ominously contained the seeds
of his later disaster as he claimed that the use of
dogs 'does rob sledge-travelling of much of its glory … no journey ever made with dogs can approach the
height of that fine conception which is realised when a party of men go forth to face hardships, dangers,
and difficulties with their own unaided efforts, and by days and weeks of hard physical labour succeed
in solving some problem of the great unknown'.

Ignoring Britain's proprietorial claim over Antarctica, the Germans, the Swedes and the French headed
south at much the same time as Scott. The German expedition was led by Erich Von Drygalski and
appeased a national pride, upset that Karl Gauss had made important contributions to the study of
terrestrial magnetism (including the location of the South Magnetic Pole) but other nations were carrying
out the field work. Fittingly, Von Drygalski's ship was called the *Gauss*. The Germans had planned well,
but the polar regions are occasionally dismissive of such things and the *Gauss* was frozen in for the
winter while still short of the Antarctic Circle. Excellent scientific work was carried out, the work including
the use of a dredge line to catch fish. The line was laid by the ingenious idea of tying it to a penguin,
then forcing the bird through a hole in the ice and ensuring it could not return and so was forced to swim
to a second hole where it, and the line, were retrieved. This seems harsh on the penguin, but not as
harsh as their use not only for dog food but as fuel for the ship's boilers. The scientists on *Gauss* also
correctly inferred the existence of the Antarctic Convergence (the narrow – 30–50 kms or 18–31 miles)
– where the warm waters of the Atlantic, Indian and Pacific Oceans meet the cold waters of the
Antarctic), though its existence was not confirmed for another 20 years. The following spring the ship
was freed from the ice in part by laying a line of rubbish across the ice, the men having noticed that the
ice melted more quickly where ash from the ship's funnel coated the ice, and reasoning, correctly, that
dark objects absorbed sunlight more readily than light ones.

The Swedish ship, the *Antarctic*, sailed late and Nordenskjöld was forced to set up camp on Snow
Hill Island to the east of the Antarctic Peninsula. Here Nordenskjöld and five others spent a hard winter
of frequent storms and bitter temperatures. When summer came Nordenskjöld and two others headed
south by dog sledge to meet the *Antarctic* at Robertson Island: they had to return when the ship did not
arrive. The ship, stopped by ice, also failed to rendezvous at Snow Hill, forcing the six men to prepare
for a second winter. Worse still, a team of three from the ship attempted to get news to Snow Hill but

right
The three men at Hope Bay built a makeshift windowless
hut and spent an unhappy winter using seal blubber for
cooking and heating so that when spring came they were
caked in thick black grease.

below
Another expedition in Antarctica at around the time of
Scott was that of Scotsman William Bruce. Bruce had
experience on whaling ships and was a leading candidate
for Scott's job. When he failed to get it he found private
sponsorship from Andrew Coats, a clothing magnate.
Bruce's expedition was highly successful. It reached
74°S, discovered Coats Land and made important studies
of penguins, but is most famous for the photograph of a
kilted Scotsman serenading a bemused penguin on the
bagpipes. What is usually omitted from the description of
this image is the fact that to keep the bird close to the
skirling pipes for the photograph one of its feet was tied
to the ice.

"Music hath Charms."
This Photo was taken off Coats Land, Lat. 74°01'S Long 22°W
discovered by the Scottish National Antarctic Expedition

could not reach it and were forced to camp at Hope Bay; and the ship failed to escape the ice, was
overcome by pressure and sank, the crew trekking across the ice to reach Paulet Island. The Swedes
were now in three overwintering groups, none of them knowing the state of the other two.

In summer 1903 they sledged towards Snow Hill and by an extraordinary coincidence met
Nordenskjöld who had sledged to James Ross Island. Approached by three black-faced men dressed in
greasy rags, Nordenskjöld was convinced he had found continental natives, his delight at meeting fellow
expedition members being tempered by the loss of a momentous discovery.

On Paulet Island five men of the remaining *Antarctic* crew made it to Hope Bay where a grimy note
directed them to Snow Hill. At the same time, concerned because the *Antarctic* was well overdue, the
Swedes sent a relief ship, as did the Argentineans. The Argentineans arrived first, reaching Snow Hill
Island where two of Nordenskjöld's men were spotted. The relieved pair and two Argentineans arrived
at the camp just hours before the Paulet party. Incredibly all three Swedish groups had met up, the
remaining men on Paulet Island being taken off as the relief ship headed north.

The French expedition aboard the *Français* was led by Dr Jean-Baptiste Charcot. It began as a private
venture, but when Charcot heard that Nordenskjöld was missing he decided to aid the rescue effort, and
the French government backed him, turning the trip into a national expedition. Learning that Nordenskjöld
was safe, the French explored the western side of the Antarctic Peninsula and wintered on Booth Island,
which forms the western side of the famous Lemaire Channel. Charcot decided against going further
south because of Britain's 'claim' over the area, a fact which endeared him to Scott but less so to the
French nation. The expedition seems to have been a happy one, but for Charcot this was tempered by
sad events. His pet pig Toby, who had happily endured the rigours of the polar winter, ate fish still
attached to the hooks used to catch them and died a miserable death, and when Charcot returned home
his wife, a granddaughter of Victor Hugo, had divorced him on the grounds of desertion.

TO THE POLE: SHACKLETON, AMUNDSEN AND SCOTT

In Britain, after his return from the *Discovery* trip, Ernest Shackleton nursed a burning desire to return, in
large part to show he was a better man than Scott whose reference to 'our invalid' in his book was
beyond Shackleton's endurance. Aware that there was little chance of being invited on another Scott
trip, Shackleton organised one of his own and in 1907 sailed south in the *Nimrod*. To his regret Edward

Wilson not only declined his invitation to join the party, but took Scott's side when he denied Shackleton use of the *Discovery* base. Worse, Wilson also sided with Scott's view that Shackleton should not go anywhere near the Ross Sea. Appalled by this, Shackleton nevertheless agreed to stay east of 170°W.

Like Scott, Shackleton visited Nansen. Scott had half-heartedly agreed to take dogs and skis after his visit, but Shackleton amazed Nansen by announcing that he would not use skis, preferring to walk, and would take ponies rather than dogs. Exactly why is disputed, but it is difficult not to see the influence of Frederick Jackson, the Englishman who had met Nansen in Franz Josef Land. Jackson had compared dogs and ponies on his expedition: the dogs had come out best every time, but mystifyingly Jackson had claimed the opposite, even telling Nansen as much (and being advised by Nansen to think again). The fact that Shackleton was planning to take a vegetarian animal to the only continent on earth where there was virtually no vegetation seems to have been subsumed by the idea that ponies represented food on the hoof, food in very large packets, food without the killing problems of dogs that upset the squeamish.

When *Nimrod* reached Antarctica, ice conditions and lack of time forced Shackleton to break his promise to Scott, though he did build a new hut at Cape Royds, 35 kms (21 miles) further from the Pole. After overwintering, Shackleton decided on two objectives: he would lead a team of four south while Edgworth David would lead a three-man team in an attempt to reach the South Magnetic Pole. Shackleton passed Scott's record southing, then forged a route up the Beardmore Glacier on to the polar plateau. Despite the misgivings of his team, all of whom were suffering exhaustion, hunger and hypothermia, Shackleton insisted on pushing on when it became clear they did not have the supplies to reach the pole. Finally, having reached 88°23'S and so being less than 160 kms (100 miles) from the pole – Shackleton's second target – the men turned around.

The return journey was a nightmare, the four on the edge of starvation for almost the whole 1,170 kms (727 miles). Several times they ran out of food altogether and only luck with the weather allowed them to reach the

right

Left to right: Adams, Wild and Shackleton at their furthest south. Realising the pole was not attainable, Shackleton forced the men on until he had reached a point less than 160 kms (100 miles) from it. Back in Britain some argued that the team's final position could not have been as far south as he claimed – the team had not taken the theodolite on their last dash to the 160 kms (100 miles) barrier – but Roald Amundsen noted that if Shackleton had travelled the same distance from the Bay of Whales, he would probably have made it all the way. It was shrewd observation.

next supply dump: bad weather would inevitably have meant death. All collapsed at some point, Eric Marshall, the team doctor, taking the lead at one stage when Shackleton fell ill. Finally arriving at the hut they found that everyone, and the *Nimrod*, had gone, but unbelievably the ship returned at just the right moment.

With the return of the ship, Shackleton found that the magnetic Pole team (David, Mawson and Mackay) had triumphed, a major success which went some way to easing his disappointment at failing to reach the Pole. Back in Britain he was given a hero's welcome and a knighthood.

Amundsen had actually intended to head for the North Pole, but news that Cook and/or Peary had reached it made him turn south. Aware that the British would cry foul and that Nansen, who had loaned him *Fram*, would be displeased as he wished to use *Fram* the following year for his own attempt to reach the South Pole, Amundsen kept his intentions secret for as long as he could. Reaching the Ross Sea he set up a base at the Bay of Whales, then used what was left of the autumn to set up bases to 82°S. When he had arrived in Antarctica, Amundsen had been 480 kms (298 miles) behind Scott. He was now, effectively, 240 kms (149 miles) ahead.

Nervous of the motorised sledges he knew Scott had, Amundsen made the mistake of setting off too early for the pole in the austral spring of 1911 and was forced to retreat by temperatures which fell to -57°C. The retreat was a shambles, the expedition being saved by Hjalmar Johansen – Nansen's companion on his northern dash from *Fram*. Johansen was furious with Amundsen who, fearing a breakdown of his leadership, sacked Johansen from the pole team. It was a bitter blow to Johansen, who already thought himself rejected by Nansen, and contributed to Johansen's suicide. That was a sad

end to a great man and it is widely believed that Amundsen felt guilty about this death, and that of Scott, for the rest of his life. Without Johansen, but with a five-man team (himself, Bjaaland, Hanssen, Hassel and Wisting) which included brilliant skiers and dog-handlers, Amundsen set out again six weeks later. The journey was almost effortless, the pole being reached on 14 December. The virgin snow there meant they had won the race with Scott. As the Norwegians returned, equally comfortably, to their base they were, sometime on 31 December, about 100 kms (62 miles) away from Scott's team which was still heading south.

Scott's team on the *Terra Nova* included Edward Wilson and several men from *Nimrod*, though others, including Wild and Mawson, declined their invitations. As Shackleton had passed 88°S using ponies, Scott also decided to use them. (When an astonished Britain heard that Amundsen was heading south, Shackleton noted that as the Norwegian was taking dogs, not ponies, he was unlikely to reach the pole as dogs 'are not very reliable'.) He also decided to use skis, but again did not take the time to learn how to use them.

Reoccupying his old base, Scott used the last of the autumn to establish southern bases, but reached only 78°28½'S because the ponies found the going hard. The motor sledges which Amundsen feared so much turned out to be all but useless. During the winter, Bowers, Cherry-Garrard and Wilson made a trip to Cape Crozier, on the east side of Ross Sea, to obtain the eggs of Emperor penguins; a round trip of some 240 kms (149 miles) formed the centrepiece of Cherry-Garrard's book *The Worst Journey in the World*, which many claim to be the finest ever written on a polar journey.

Scott started his journey with support teams which returned to base when they had laid supplies for

above

Scott's team at the South Pole. Bowers, seated left, is pulling the string which operates the camera shutter. Scott, standing centre, clearly shows the disappointment of coming second.

right

Scott's final camp. The bodies of Scott, Wilson and Bowers were found in the tent when it was discovered the following spring. Left in place, the bodies will one day complete the journey from the Pole to the sea (or perhaps they already have).

the return or passed them to those continuing. At the bottom of the Beardmore Glacier the last of the ponies was shot, leaving Scott and 11 men to manhaul the rest of the way. Four men returned from the top of the glacier, the last group returning from the polar plateau. At that point Scott decided to continue with a team of five rather than four, throwing both his own team and the last to return into confusion, particularly as the man he decided to take, Bowers, had already, on instructions, left his skis behind. The Pole team therefore had four men on skis and one on foot.

On 16 January the men detected something ahead: it was one of Amundsen's black flags, the surrounding snow etched with ski and sledge marks, and paw prints. The British had lost the race, Scott's diary revealing the anguish of defeat and failure. Though Scott undoubtedly made mistakes and so contributed to his own downfall, it is hard not to have sympathy for him and his team as they stood in the desolation of the plateau staring at the Norwegian tent.

The return journey turned into a nightmare as the weather and fatigue slowed the party to a deathly pace. Edgar Evans was the first to die, falling

down into the snow and failing to stand again. Laurence Oates was next, taking his frostbitten feet out into a blizzard with the words 'I am just going outside and may be some time'. (Scott recorded these words, though Wilson, writing to Oates' mother, does not mention them.) The last three men, Scott, Wilson and Henry Bowers, struggled on until they were 17.5 km (13 miles) from a supply dump. Scott was now finished, his frostbitten right foot probably gangrenous. The other two tried to continue but were driven back by the weather. The three then waited, apparently patiently, for death, Scott penning his famous, poignant last letters. The tent, with the three still inside their sleeping bags, was discovered in November 1912 by a British search party. They were buried where they lay.

LATER EXPEDITIONS

While Amundsen and Scott were racing for the Pole there were three other expeditions on Antarctica: Japanese explorers under Nobu Shirase, German explorers under Wilhelm Filchner and the Australasian Antarctic Expedition led by Douglas Mawson. Of these, the most significant was that of Mawson, if only because of its harrowing tale of survival.

Mawson was hoping to fill the gaps on the map between McMurdo and the German discoveries of 1902. He hoped to land close to Cape Adare, but the unforgiving terrain forced him much further west, to Cape Denison in Commonwealth Bay.

above

Mawson's choice of Cape Denison was unfortunate as it is one of the windiest places on the continent, cold, dense air accelerating under the influence of gravity to speeds of over 300 kms/hr as it falls from the high Antarctic plateau. The persistence of these katabatic winds (named from the Greek for 'going downhill') only became apparent to Mawson when it was too late.

During the winter some supplies were placed in an excavated ice cavern called Aladdin's Cave in readiness for the teams that set out when summer came. One of the exploration teams comprised Mawson, Belgrave Ninnis, a British army officer, and Xavier Mertz, a Swiss lawyer and mountaineer. The three men headed east, soon finding that the going was made dangerous by huge crevasses, their dog teams often falling into these holes. Each time they were retrieved until, disastrously, Ninnis and his dog team disappeared into a vast crevasse and were lost.

Mawson and Mertz immediately set off for Cape Denison 500 km (310 miles) away. Feeding the weakest dogs to the strongest, but soon eating dog flesh themselves, the men moved as fast as the terrain would allow. When killing the dogs they noticed that, even when emaciated, the animals' livers were large: soon these livers formed most of the men's diet. But the livers had high concentrations of Vitamin A, a poison in large

above
Mawson and Mertz peered into the crevasse for some sign of Ninnis or his sledge. The loss of the sledge meant that all the dog food and most of the men's food was lost.

doses, and soon both men were suffering from dysentery and nausea, loss of hair and skin, and chronic stomach pain. These symptoms lead ultimately to delirium, convulsions and death – as it did for Mertz, after Mawson, the younger, fitter man, gave him extra rations in the hope of prolonging his survival.

Mawson buried Mertz, cut a sledge in half with a penknife and continued alone, skin peeling from his thighs and scrotum requiring him to walk bow-legged. The entire soles of his feet then came away, forcing him to bandage them in place to ease the pain of the raw, exposed new flesh. His entire body seemed to be rotting away. As his progress slowed, his hair began to fall out and he feared the onset of scurvy. There was also the fear that his team mates might abandon him and retreat before winter arrived. Finally he reached a cairn where there was food and the desperate news that a rescue party had left just six hours earlier. To continue, Mawson had to improvise crampons to cope with hard, polished ice, knocking nails into pieces of wood which he strapped to his feet. The nails forced their way back, piercing his boots and flesh. He was now exhausted, both physically and mentally, the nearness of rescue bringing its own despair. He reached Aladdin's Cave, but a blizzard imprisoned him there for a week. When the weather cleared he saw the smoke of a disappearing ship and realised he might have to spend the winter alone. But some men had stayed, and came to meet him. So appalling was his condition that the first to reach him asked 'Which one are you?'

In Britain the national grief over Scott's death had been replaced, at government level, by cold reality. Europe was heading towards war and Britain did not want the expense of another southern expedition.

above top

The *Endurance* frozen in at 76°35'S. As well as his famous series of black and white prints Frank Hurley, the expedition's photographer, took a small number of 'Paget' plates, an early form of colour photography which used dyed screens to produce a basic colour image. The cost and the fact that enlargements showed the screen

pattern meant the technique never caught on. It is difficult to produce a colour image from Hurley's original plates, but they do offer a fascinating view of Shackleton's expedition.

above

Another of Hurley's Paget plates. This one shows Ernest Shackleton watching a lead form in the Weddell Sea.

This forced Ernest Shackleton, still wanting to leave his mark on Antarctica, to seek private funds for his proposed traverse of the continent from the Weddell to the Ross seas. His ship, *Endurance*, left Britain on 1 August 1914. On 4 August Britain declared war on Germany. Shackleton offered his services to the war effort, but was told to continue. Today the expedition is seen as triumphant, but it is worth remembering that at the time there were many who thought that brave, fit men should have been heading towards, not away from, the conflict.

The story of the *Endurance* is now so well known it does not require a long retelling. Shackleton's attempt to reach the coast of the Weddell Sea was thwarted by the ice which first held, then sank his ship. Forced to abandon their attempted traverse, the team drifted north on the sea-ice, then used the ship's boats to reach the hostile, uninhabited Elephant Island. From there Shackleton and five others made what is still considered to be the most remarkable sea journey of all time, taking an open boat across the raging Southern Ocean to reach South Georgia. Not only was this journey remarkable for the tenacity of the crew, who spent 16 days on the crossing, but for the feat of navigation by Frank Worsley, the captain of the *Endurance*. South Georgia's barely explored and uninhabited southern coast was reached, the landing proving as fraught as the crossing. Shackleton, with two others, then had to cross the unexplored glacial heart of the island to reach the whaling station at Stromness. From there he set out to rescue those left on Elephant Island.

The journey of the *Endurance* and her crew was recorded by Frank Hurley, a brilliant photographer, whose shots helped the trip become a legend of survival against the odds. But it is rarely mentioned that *Endurance* was only half the expedition, the other half going to the Ross Sea in order to lay supply dumps for Shackleton's expected traverse. This expedition was far less successful, resulting in the deaths of three men. The supply dumps they prepared were also far from adequate and, had Shackleton succeeded in reaching the shores of the Weddell Sea, he would have been lucky to survive the traverse.

The world that Shackleton and his men returned to had changed, almost beyond their imagining. The

above

Pipe in hand, Frank Wild contemplates the wreck of the *Endurance*. One of Frank Hurley's remarkable series of photos of the expedition.

below

Shackleton, Peary and Amundsen. On 16 November 1913 the three greatest polar explorers of the age were entertained at the Bellevue Stratford Hotel, Philadelphia.

war which would be 'over by Christmas' was grinding on. Shackleton's reception was less rapturous than the one his name now elicits: on the Falklands one islander commented that he should have 'been at the war long ago instead of messing about on icebergs'. Back in Britain his men were called up for active service: Tim McCarthy, who had survived the open boat journey, was killed within four months of reaching South Georgia. Shackleton, too old for active service, was now something of an anachronism. In 1920 he decided to go south again. He had no clear objective: perhaps he just wanted to be in a place where he felt less out of touch. At South Georgia he had a massive heart attack and died.

After Shackleton's trip, journeys to the Antarctic were mainly to fill in the gaps in the map of the continent. It soon became apparent that using planes speeded this process, and also allowed a new generation to adventure among the frozen wastes. Englishman Hubert Wilkins and American Ben Eielson made the first Antarctic flight from Deception Island in 1928, the first flight over the continent itself being the following year, from the Little America base at the Bay of Whales, by Richard Byrd and his pilot Bernt Balchen. Byrd, whose claim to have been the first man to fly to the North Pole has since been discredited, then made the first flight over the South Pole. In 1933 Byrd returned with an even bigger expedition, his planes exploring a vast tract of Antarctica, though the expedition was chiefly notable for Byrd's decision to overwinter alone in a hut inland from his base. This feat of solitary endurance almost ended in disaster when fumes from a faulty petrol-driven generator poisoned him. Alarmed by his increasingly erratic radio messages the base team mounted a rescue, arriving just in time to save his life.

The next flyer on the continent was Lincoln Ellsworth, who had made Arctic flights with Amundsen and Nobile. Ellsworth came south in 1933 determined to add a trans-Antarctic flight to his Arctic record. He

was unsuccessful in 1933 and again in 1934 (when, during the journey home his ship was overrun by rats which not only ate all the expedition's boats and snowshoe webbing but also killed and ate the ship's cat). In 1935 he tried again, this time succeeding in flying the length of the Antarctic Peninsula and on to the Ross Sea.

After the 1939-45 war, as part of the International Geographical Year (IGY) the Americans set up a base at the South Pole, one which remains to this day. On 31 October 1956 a DC3 landed at the Pole and Admiral George Dufek became the eleventh man, and the first American, to stand there. As part of the IGY the British decided to realise Shackleton's dream of crossing Antarctica from the Weddell to the Ross. In charge of the project was Vivian Fuchs who was to lead a team from the Weddell to the Ross, using supply depots beyond the Pole, laid down by a New Zealand team under Sir Edmund Hillary who, three years earlier, had, with Tenzing Norgay, been first to Everest's summit. The Fuchs team overwintered on the shores of the Weddell in 1956, Hillary's team using part of the winter to repeat the 'Worst Journey in the World' to test his vehicles.

Fuchs's team found the going difficult, especially getting his vehicles on to the plateau, but once established there things went better, his US SnoCats performing well. On the other side of the continent

above
Ellsworth's plane *Polar Star* slipping through the ice after being unloaded from his ship (the *Wyatt Earp*) in 1933. The anticipated flights had to be abandoned.

right
Ed Hillary's vehicles for the Trans-Antarctic expedition were standard Ferguson tractors with added tracks and a modified cab. Here Hillary tries out a standard, but trackless, tractor in New Zealand prior to the trip. His team, presumably gathered (in expedition clothing) to be impressed by the demonstration, appear either baffled or completely underwhelmed.

Hillary laid down his depots and then waited for Fuchs, the plan being that he would lead him to the Ross-side base. With Fuchs behind schedule Hillary decided to press on, and on 4 January 1958 his team reached the Pole, the first men to do so overland since Scott in 1912. This journey caused considerable friction between Hillary and Fuchs, the latter believing (almost certainly correctly) that it was an attempt to steal his thunder. However, the argument, which even reached prime ministerial level, did not stop Hillary returning to the Pole to join in the welcome for Fuchs when his team finally arrived two weeks later. Fuchs then continued along Hillary's outward route, accomplishing the first Antarctic traverse in March.

In 1980 the Trans-Globe expedition, the three-man British team of Charles Burton (whose death at the age of 59 was announced as this book was being written), Sir Ranulph Fiennes and Oliver Sheppard (none with Antarctic experience) landed on the Queen Maud Land coast, close to the 0° meridian. The expedition was intending to circumnavigate the earth along (or as close as possible to) the prime meridian and, as part of that trip, was intending to cross Antarctica using open snow scooters, a feat which many claimed was not possible because of the extremes of cold and wind the continent experiences. Despite the cold the men succeeded, reaching the Pole on 15 December and Scott base on Ross Island on 11 January 1981. They had achieved the second crossing of the continent, covering 4,200 kms (2,600 miles) in 66 days.

The next land journey to the Pole, in 1985–86, recreated the journey of Scott's team. 'In the Footsteps of Scott' was the brainchild of Briton Robert Swan and was intended to reproduce, as far as possible, Scott's journey, Swan even transporting his team to the start by ship. The team recreated the 'Worst Journey in the World' by manhauling to Cape Crozier, then, almost exactly duplicating Scott's route, three men – Swan with Roger Mear and Gareth Wood – set off for the Pole. They took no radio so as to recreate the same sense of isolation, but had sledges that weighed only half as much – in part because they were not walking out (they had their own air transport), in part because modern foodstuffs and equipment are lighter. Having set out on the same date as Scott they arrived at the Pole on 11 January 1986, a week ahead of Scott's schedule. In another parallel with Scott's trip they arrived to bad news: their ship had sunk. To make matters worse they also had a hostile reception from the Americans, much as several later expeditions have done. Officially this is because the Americans fear having to risk men and resources rescuing idiot adventurers, but it is difficult not to see an element of proprietorial rights in the antagonism.

The 'Footsteps' expedition was the last which used a ship for transport (though the use of a ship was a choice rather than a necessity). The air age had truly arrived with the discovery, at Patriot Hills near

above top
Hillary (left) and Fuchs (right) are greeted at the South Pole by Admiral George Dufek.

above
British explorers Ranulph Fiennes (left) and Charles Burton tidying up the Trans-Globeship before a ceremony to mark the end of the three years, 56,000 km (35,000 miles) expedition. Sadly Charles Burton's death was announced while this book was in preparation.

the south-western edge of the Ronne Ice Shelf, of a natural blue-ice runway which could be used safely by wheeled (as opposed to ski-mounted) aircraft. Using this base, and then a light aircraft to fly to the shore of the Weddell Sea, Reinhold Messner, the world's greatest high-altitude climber, and the German Arved Fuchs repeated the British traverse by Vivian Fuchs (no relation to Arved), using specially designed parawings to assist with the towing of their sledges. This was the first non-mechanical traverse, Shackleton's dream if not his method.

At Patriot Hills, Messner and Fuchs met the team which was making the longest traverse possible on Antarctica. The six-man team – American Will Steger, Frenchman Jean-Louis Etienne, Victor Boyarsky, a Russian scientist, Qin Dahe, a Chinese glaciologist, and two dog experts, the Japanese Keizo Funatsu and Briton Geoff Somers – started near the tip of the Antarctic Peninsula, reached the pole and continued to the Russian Mirny Station on the shore of the Davis Sea, a distance of 6,000 km (3,725 miles) using dog sledges and moving between a dozen previously laid-down supply depots as well as being re-supplied by air from Patriot Hills.

Despite these successes, the idea of an unsupported traverse of the continent remained elusive, having been attempted several times (including a couple of near misses by Briton Ranulf Fiennes and his partners). One target was achieved in 1993–94 when the Norwegian Erling Kagge made the first unsupported, solo journey to the Pole from Berkner Island. Not until three years later was the first unsupported traverse achieved by another Norwegian, Børge Ousland, the outstanding polar explorer of the age. Since that time there have been other traverses, each lengthening the traverse line, until in the austral summer of 2000–2001 the Norwegians Rolf Bae and Eirik Sønneland completed a distance of 3,800 kms (2,360 miles), the longest unsupported journey ever made. The pair started out from Queen Maud, trekking for 105 days to reach McMurdo base – a phenomenal achievement but one which the lure of the southern continent will doubtless see surpassed at some future time.

Peaks

When man began to climb mountains is a question to which there are several answers depending upon how the word 'climb' is defined. The discovery of 'Oetzi', the Copper Age hunter, high in the Alps implies that men were certainly going into the mountains over 5,000 years ago: but that was a search for food which involved a climb. And the soldiers of Alexander needed to climb the Sogdian Rock in 327BC in order to force the ascent and inflict defeat on Oxyartes. In 1280 Peter III, King of Aragon, climbed Canigou, the prominent peak at the eastern end of the Pyrenees. His ascent does at least have the merits of having been completed for no better reason than Canigou being claimed the highest peak in his realm. Sadly, the fact that the king said he found a lake on the summit, one in which a dragon lived, implies that his ascent owed more to fervent desire than actuality, especially as the idea that dragons lived on mountain tops was one that was widely believed.

Half a century later, in 1336, the poet Petrarch climbed Mont Ventoux and then wrote about the climb and the summit view in a lyrical passage that has hardly been bettered as an expression of the aesthetic joy of climbing.

In the same century several other peaks were climbed, some for scientific reasons, but many for reasons that had more to do with satisfying the human spirit than with any purely practical idea. Evidence of this was found in the grim discovery of the frozen corpses of children, close to the summit of Llullaillaco, a 6,723m (22,713 ft) mountain in northern Argentina: the three children are believed to have been human sacrifices by the Inca priesthood, perhaps 500 years ago.

And now, in the 21st century, Mount Kailas is still regarded as a sacred mountain by the Tibetans. There is something about mountains which touches the need for spirituality in many human beings and inspires the need to reach their summits in many more.

MONT BLANC

Given that it is impossible to identify the true beginnings of mountaineering, many regard the first ascent of Mont Blanc as the start. The top was first reached on 8 August 1786 by Michel-Gabriel Paccard, a Chamonix doctor, and Jacques Balmat, a crystal hunter. This unlikely duo were thrown together by a reward offered by Geneva-born Horace Bénédict de Saussure, a man of independent means. Saussure's desire to see Mont Blanc climbed was driven by the belief that a route to the top of the highest peak in the Alps would be a highway to a better understanding of science. Interestingly, though his climbing of other peaks suggests he was a fit man in his younger days, Saussure had no interest in finding the route to the top. Instead he offered a reward to the first man to do so, and waited. He waited 25 years before the right team found a successful way up the peak and claimed his reward. Only then did Saussure decide to climb the mountain himself. In 1787 he did so, accompanied by Balmat and a caravan of 18 guides who laboured under the weight of a folding bed and a variety of scientific instruments. Over the next 60 or so years other Alpine peaks were climbed, though in almost all cases the drive to climb them was the thirst for knowledge rather than a desire for adventure. All that changed in the 1850s with the arrival of the British and the Golden Age of alpine climbing.

right

Mountaineers on Mont Blanc during the early years of the 20th century. Equipment and technique had not changed much since the 'Golden Age' a half-century before.

The ascent of the Matterhorn defines the closing of the Golden Age, but it is more difficult to be quite so specific with the opening date. In 1851 Albert Smith, the son of a surgeon, and a regular contributor to the humorous UK magazine *Punch*, joined three Oxford undergraduates in an ascent of Mont Blanc. The four young men had 16 guides, and were also accompanied on the initial part of the climb by a further 20 men who carried the supplies thought necessary for the undertaking. As these supplies included 90 bottles of wine, two of champagne and three of cognac, 11 large and 35 small fowls, 20 loaves of bread, together with quantities of mutton, veal and beef, it can be seen both why the porters were necessary and that the chief purpose of the expedition was not scientific. To be fair to the young Britons it seems that the guides had taken advantage of their youth to ensure their own good time. With that proviso it is clear that with the arrival of the British, the climbing of mountains had become a pastime.

THE GOLDEN AGE

Monte Rosa, the second highest peak of the Alps, has an array of distinct summits laid out along a sinuous ridge. After Mont Blanc had been climbed, the ascent of Monte Rosa became the grail of climbers and over a period of years the summits were picked off, the great clefts which separated the peaks meaning that the 'soft option' of reaching one peak and traversing the ridge which linked them was not available. Only in 1855, when three local guides led an English party which included Charles Hudson to the summit of the Dufourspitze, the highest summit, was Monte Rosa finally climbed. The climb of the Dufourspitze could be claimed the first of the Golden Age, though some of those who took part had already begun an assault on the high Alpine peaks which would see virtually all of them climbed in the years to 1865.

The increase in interest in climbing led, on 22 December 1857, to the formation of the Alpine Club in London, its first president being John Ball, a Dublin-born botanist. Ball, who published important works on the flora of the European Alps, Morocco and South America, was also the editor of the Club's first publication, *Peaks, Passes and Glaciers*, which appeared in 1859 to critical acclaim. After he had resigned the presidency in 1860, he published his three-volume *Ball's Alpine Guides* between 1863 and 1868. In these he suggested the building of hotels and mountain huts, a fact which did much to popularise the area. Other early members of the British wave that swept the Alps included Leslie Stephen, John Tyndall and Douglas Freshfield. Stephen is most famous as the father of Virginia Woolf, but that is to ignore his contribution to climbing and mountain literature. He was a brilliant writer, as anyone who has read *The Playground of Europe*, his book on his alpine journeys, will know. Stephen loved mountains, caring little for the competitive edge that sometimes underwrote attempts at new peaks, nor for the idea that the hills should be visited purely for the advancement of science. His

above
John Ball, first President of the Alpine Club. Ball's guides to the Alps started a wave of interest in the area and led to the building of many of the hotels still used by visitors.

above

Francis Fox Tuckett. Tuckett is an interesting climber if for no other reason than the fact that his remarkable record of climbs is matched by his astonishing ability to survive, his career including a seemingly endless number of narrow escapes from lightning strikes, avalanches (he was inches away from being annihilated by what is often claimed to have been the biggest-ever avalanche on the Eiger) and rock falls. He was also twice arrested as a spy when his mountain wanderings took him over the high border between Hapsburg Austria and the emerging Italian state.

conflict with scientist John Tyndall over the latter led to Tyndall resigning from the Alpine Club in disgust. Tyndall was a fervent believer in the idea that the advancement of science was the only true reason for climbing. His climbing achievements included the first ascent of the Weisshorn in 1861: his scientific achievements include the answering of the deceptively straightforward question as to why the sky is blue. Douglas Freshfield, a one-time President of the Royal Geographical Society, later extended climbing's horizons by visiting Africa's Ruwenzori, climbing Mount Elbrus in the Caucasus and, famously, circumnavigating Kangchenjunga, the giant peak of Indian Sikkim and the world's third-highest mountain. Francis Fox Tuckett joined Freshfield to explore the Brenta Dolomites, extending the British influence eastwards. The same pair were also the first to traverse the Pale di San Martino, the largest of the Dolomite groups, in 1865. Tuckett also made the first ascent of the Civetta and of the Marmolada di Rocco (the lower of the Marmolada's two summits) with John Ball.

But by far the most famous of the group of British climbers who contributed to the ascents of the Golden Age was Edward Whymper. Whymper was an engraver, socially inferior to the scientists and those of independent means who made up the British alpinists. But soon after his first visit, he was able to mix with them, his abilities and drive as a climber placing him on a par. Although he made important climbs – for instance the first ascents of the Barre des Ecrins, the Aiguille Verte and Aiguille d'Argentière – Whymper's name will always be associated with the Matterhorn. He attempted the peak nine times and was initially in competition with Tyndall for the first ascent (the competition between them did not stop their behaving like civilised men: when Tyndall's book *Hours of Exercise in the Alps* was published in 1871 it was Whymper who produced the illustrations). Later, Whymper tired of his guide Jean-Antoine Carrel and, on the final, fateful Matterhorn climb, was in competition with him too. Carrel, an Italian nationalist, wanted the peak climbed from the Italian side, a further conflict as Whymper eventually realised that the Swiss side offered the easier route.

Whymper set out from Zermatt for the successful climb. At the same time Carrel was trying again from the Italian side, while Tyndall was also preparing for another attempt, again from Italy. The composition of Whymper's team has been discussed ever since the climb. There were three guides, Michel Croz, Peter Taugwalder ('old Peter') and his son 'young Peter'. Croz was good, old Peter not very good and his son inexperienced. As well as Whymper, there were also Charles Hudson, Lord Francis Douglas and Douglas Hadow. Hudson, as noted earlier, had been on the first ascent of Monte Rosa, but the other two were inexperienced. Douglas was just 18 years old, though he was a climber of promise. Hadow was 19, and much less promising.

The ascent went well and from the summit they were able to see Carrel and his team about 400m (1,312 ft) below. Whymper's team hurled stones down to attract attention: such behaviour on a mountain is guaranteed also to attract abuse. Seeing Whymper's party at the summit, the Italians retreated. The

below
The Matterhorn, the most famous and most photogenic of Alpine peaks. It stands in an isolated position, the more impressive for being so, above the lovely Swiss village of Zermatt. But its shape is a little misleading: only from the Zermatt side is the Matterhorn so beautiful. From other angles it is nowhere nearly as perfect.

above
Edward Whymper. Whymper blamed the accident on the use of a thin, weak rope which had snapped when the fall occurred. Had a stronger rope been used, he implied, the accident would not have happened. He claimed to have been a long way off when the party roped up for the descent, an attempt to absolve himself of responsibility for the use of the rope and, therefore, for the accident. Not everyone was convinced, blaming Whymper for the party being both too large and inexperienced for such a climb.

victorious team also retreated; and during the descent came the fateful slip. Hadow fell, knocking off Croz, who was below him. The two dragged Hudson and Douglas down. Between these four and the remaining three was a piece of old rope. Whymper, alerted by Croz's startled cry, braced himself and held the fall long enough for this rope to snap between Douglas and old Peter. Four men then fell silently to their doom leaving the surviving three paralysed with shock. It is a credit to Whymper's abilities that he got them down safely. In Britain the accident was headline news, though the accusations and counter-accusations did nothing to deter Whymper's ambitions as a climber. He later climbed in the Caucasus and, teaming up with Carrel again, went to the Andes. The pair even climbed the Matterhorn together in 1874, old rivalries finally put to bed.

With the Matterhorn climbed, the Golden Age ended. It was not so much that tragedy affected climbers but that there were very few peaks left to attempt, the climbing world having to move on. The British had guides to accompany them, but the future lay with men whose ambitions would carry them beyond the capabilities of local guides and into a new era.

above
Italian climber Riccardo Cassin, one of the finest climbers of the inter-war years. Cassin was involved in the first ascents of two of the six Great North Faces. His climbing career continued into old age; in 1975 at the age of 66 he led an expedition to the formidable south face of Lhotse in the Himalaya.

NORTH FACE

Climbing with local guides was expensive – one reason why the rich, leisured British upper class dominated the sport – and so was not available to a new generation of adventurers who wanted to experience the thrill of climbing. With the notable exception of Albert Mummery, who helped pioneer the change to guideless climbing, the new generation were those who could more easily afford to travel to the Alps for the simple reason that they lived closer.

The Matterhorn accident also revolutionised the techniques of climbing. Before 1865 the use of the rope for protection was rudimentary. The accident showed the rope's true value. Greater emphasis on ropework led, inevitably, to the development of belays, running belays and the hardware that these require. And the level of protection against death and serious injury created the confidence to venture on to steep ground, dismissed as unclimbable by the early alpinists.

Georg Winkler, a diminutive German, (he was just 1.5m – 4 feet 11 inches – tall) had a meteoric career as the Golden Age was ending, climbing improbable rock spires in the Dolomites as a teenager. He invariably climbed solo, and fell to his death aged only 18 years in 1888. In 1899 the famed Campanile Basso in the Brenta Dolomites was climbed by the Germans Ampferer and Berger. It was probably the hardest climb in Europe at the time. The east face of the same tower was climbed solo in 1911 by Paul Preuss in what many still regard as one of the greatest climbs of all time. In the same year pitons were used for the first time by the Italian Angelo Dibona on a climb in the Karwendel. After the 1914–18 war had halted the advance of standards – as well as taking a toll of the potential climbers – the German Emil Solleder pushed standards forward again, climbing what is now regarded as the first Grade 6 climb in the Alps. Solleder was not alone: Armand Charlet and Pierre Allain from France, Hans Lauper from Switzerland, Italy's Emilio Comici and Riccardo Cassin, and another German, Willo Welzenbach, were similarly pushing at the borders of the possible. The British also produced the occasional brilliant climber. Geoffrey Winthrop Young was perhaps the best of these. He lost a leg in the 1914–18 war but did not allow that to cause him much inconvenience, climbing the Matterhorn with a wooden one.

Against this backdrop of increasing standards and levels of protection it was inevitable that eyes would turn to the greatest faces in the Alps. The geography of the area means that these are invariably the north faces, the fact that these see less of the sun adding an additional element of gloom to steep, forbidding walls. The climbing world rapidly decided that there were six North Faces which stood above all others in terms of difficulty and commitment. Not surprisingly the names of the leading climbers of the day are associated with them.

above

The North Face of the
Eiger. The position of the
face, rearing up from
Alpine meadows above
the famous rack railway
which takes visitors from
Grindelwald to Kleine
Scheidegg and then
down to Murren, means
that dramas are played
out in front of an
audience of thousands.

The first to fall was the North Face of the Matterhorn which was climbed in 1931 by the relatively unknown Schmid brothers. At the time, the leading German climber was Willo Welzenbach whose climbs on the north faces of the Gross Weissbachhorn, the Grands Charmoz and some Bernese Oberland faces were the hardest climbs of the late 1920s/early 1930s. Had he survived the nightmare of Nanga Parbat in 1934 he would doubtless have been a contender on the later North Faces. As it was, the Cime Grande di Lavaredo fell to the Italian Comici in 1933 while Riccardo Cassin captured the Badile and Grandes Jorasses (Pointe Walke) North Faces in 1937 and 1938 respectively. The fifth face, that of the Dru, was climbed in 1935 by Pierre Allain. The last of the great North Faces to be climbed was also the most sought after, the most famous and the most infamous, the North Face of the Eiger.

The notoriety of the Eiger is due, in large part, to its position. Rising from the meadows of the Bernese Oberland, the Eiger stands above a scene which could hardly be a greater contrast to that of the climbers on its north face. In summer, walkers wander across meadows of alpine flowers, the only sound being the tinkling of cow bells. In winter, skiers scud across the same fields before reaching woods where snow sparkling on the trees offers a scene repeated on endless Christmas cards. At all times, trains chug up the steep line between Grindelwald and Kleine Scheidegg. All this can be seen and heard by the climbers on the wall. And there is a powerful telescope at Scheidegg which allows people to watch life and death struggles played out before their eyes. On the early attempts it was death that held centre stage. Two young Germans attacked the wall at the centre of its base in 1935. They were watched as they made their way slowly up. Their progress became slower, then stopped. Cloud now drifted across the face, obscuring their final moments.

Worse was to come the following year when two Austrians and two Germans made another attempt. They started at the right edge of the wall, the young German Anderl Hinterstoisser finding the key traverse to reach the centre of the face. The traverse now bears his name, but it was to prove to be not only the

below

Henirich Harrer pictured in Delhi in 1951 after his escape from Lhasa. In his youth Harrer had been an exceptional skier, and a member of the Austrian Olympic team in 1936. In 1938 he was one of the four man team that climbed the North Wall of the Eiger. In 1939 he was invited to join the German Nanga Parbat expedition. The team members were interned in British India when war was declared. With others he escaped, making his way to Tibet where he became a close companion of the young Dalai Lama, with whom he fled in 1950, when the Chinese invaded.

key which opened the door to the route up the face, but the one which closed the door as well, the four young men being trapped when they were forced to retreat after one of the Austrians was injured by a falling stone. All attempts to reverse the traverse failed and, eventually, there was an accident. Three men were killed instantly, but the fourth, Toni Kurz, survived. His long drawn-out death, as he tried to climb down, came with his frostbitten, exhausted body finally succumbing just metres away from a rescue party, the agony played out in full view of the crowds and reporters watching from below. Eiger Nordwand, the German name of the face, was translated into Eiger Mordwand, the death wall, the murder wall. Things were not improved by the demise the following year of two Italians. Eight had now lost their lives and the wall had acquired a reputation that lives on today.

The Eiger was finally climbed in 1938 by the Germans Anderl Heckmair, Ludwig Vörg and Heinrich Harrer, and the Austrian Fritz Kasperak. Even that ascent was not without controversy. Adolf Hitler saw the climb as a triumph of the Germanic peoples and met the climbers. The argument over whether the climb was inspired by nationalism has never gone away and was brought into sharp focus by revelations about Harrer's past when the film of his book *Seven Years in Tibet* was released a few years ago. The face was not climbed again until 1947, and had had only 50 ascents by the mid-1960s. As an interesting statistic, the fiftieth climb was by a woman, Daisy Voog, the first female ascent. Interspersed with the successful ascent were more tragedies, all played out in front of the Scheidegg telescope. Worst of all perhaps was that in 1957, when an Italian was left hanging from ropes and two young Germans disappeared. A second Italian was rescued from the face, and that rescue and the lonely death of his partner again made for headline news and ghoulish watching.

The Eiger has continued to play a prominent role in the development of the Alps, despite the standard route now being considered one of the easiest climbs on the vast wall (though caution is required when suggesting as much; easiest should not be read as 'easy': when the weather turns bad, it is still a major undertaking and the death toll continues to mount). The level of difficulty achieved by those at the top of the sport has, of course, been pushed upwards, though it is now chiefly climbers rather than newspaper readers who recognise the latest hard lines. Yet, it is the peaks of the great north faces which attract attention. In 1952 the west face of the Dru was climbed by a French team. Then in 1955 the Italian Walter Bonatti achieved what is widely believed to be the greatest feat of Alpine mountaineering by soloing a new route on the Dru. In 1965 he celebrated the centenary of the Matterhorn's first ascent by soloing a new route on the north face, this time in winter. Further advances were made on the Eiger (International team, 1966), Direct Grandes Jorasses (René Desmaisson, The Shroud, 1968) and on the Dru (Cecchinel/Jaeger, 1973 and Destivelle, 1991).

Today's climbers, though pushing standards even further, have also returned to the great faces to reduce the amount of aid used, climbing the old routes in the new style. They have also brought the techniques acquired in the Alps to the world's greater ranges. In 1954 a French team pushed a route up the imposing south face of Aconcagua, and then in 1985 the Pole Wojciech Kurtyka and the German Robert Schauer climbed the west face of Gasherbrum IV in the Karakoram. This, and the route on the north face of Thalay Sagar in the Garwhal Himal by the Hungarians Dékàny and Ozvàth, are regarded by most experts as the finest high-altitude climbs to have been accomplished to date.

above left
The successful Eiger North Wall team with Hitler. Left to right are Anderl Heckmair, Heinrich Harrer, Hitler, Fritz Kasparek, Ludwig Vörg, together with Herr von Tschamer-Osten and Wilhelm Frick. Vörg's arm is bandaged because it had been badly punctured by Harrer's crampons when he fell during the climb. It was natural for Hitler to take advantage of the success of the Austrian-German team's success on the Eiger and, in pre-war Germany, for the climbers (young and unworldly) to accept the attention. Only after the war was the cynical nature of the meeting seized upon in an attempt to question the motives of the four men. The photograph now makes uneasy viewing, particularly when it is recalled that Frick, the 'Protector' of Bohemia was executed for war crimes after the Nuremburg trials.

above
Catherine Destivelle, the foremost woman mountaineer of her generation.

above

El Capitan in California's Yosemite Valley, one of the biggest yet most accessible rock faces on earth. The face has been the scene of many significant advances in rock-climbing technique.

opposite

Lynn Hill laybacking beneath the Great Roof on El Capitan's Nose in 1993. With the British climber Simon Nadin, Lynn almost completed the first free ascent of this famous climb, the pair having to finish the last few pitches of the route using aid when they ran out of food. Lynn returned a short while later with American climber Brooke Sandahl and completed the climb. Each of these climbs had taken several days. Later, Lynn repeated the climb with American Steve Sutton in a single day. The free ascent of the Great Roof has one of the main challenges on the climb. Lynn is laybacking, a technique which uses hands and feet in opposition.

ON THE ROCKS

Many of the advances used to improve standards in the Alps were developed in rock climbing, a sport which differs from alpinism in the scale of the faces being climbed. Pure rock climbers may take as long on a 30m (98 ft) route as their alpine counterparts do on a great north face. In the USA's Yosemite Valley the two ideas blended together with the development of techniques which allowed the vast, sheer faces of granite found there to be climbed. The first major climb was in 1950 on Sentinel Rock, but the most famous such climb was the ascent of the Nose on El Capitan by Warren Harding's team in 1958. The climb took 45 days over an 18-month period and involved the use of 675 pitons and 125 expansion bolts.

Other faces were climbed, newer generations of climbers not only doing their own routes, but attempting to reduce the amount of aid on the older climbs. It soon became the norm to do climbs such as the Nose in one push. The time to climb the route tumbled. In 1975 it was done in a day. By 2001 this had been reduced to less than four hours.

At the same time as climbers were trying to reduce the time, others were trying to climb the route free — that is with no artificial aids. This was finally achieved by Lynn Hill and Brooke Sandahl over two days in 1993. Lynn Hill later returned to establish another milestone by completing a free ascent in one day.

The techniques the Americans learned on the great Yosemite faces were transferred to Europe, a four-man team climbing the south face of the Fou in 1963. Not that the Europeans were far behind in terms of rock-climbing ability, or in the speed with which they acquired the new techniques. In Britain, after the 1939–45 war rock climbing standards were advanced by a generation of rock climbers whose roots were in the working class of northern England rather than in the university class that had dominated the pre-war sport. Joe Brown and Don Whillans led the advance, Whillans later transferring his skills to the Himalayas. Brown dominated British rock climbing for two decades, an unprecedented reign in so competitive a sport.

In rock climbing, the turn-over at the top is similar to that in pop music, a comparison that seemed

below

Trango Towers. The Towers form part of the left (north-eastern) ridge of the Trango Glacier which flows into the lower part of the Baltoro Glacier in the Karakoram. The techniques of modern rock climbing have been transferred to the Towers, despite their being over 6,000m (19,685 ft) high.

even more appropriate when climbing became the new rock-and-roll in the final decades of the 20th century. With state-of-the-art equipment and a fitness and technique developed with the help of indoor climbing walls, the standard of rock climbing shot up. With these advantages available to all, and cheap transport allowing almost anyone to reach the great walls of Yosemite and the Alps, as well as those of Patagonia and the Himalayas, climbing was no longer the preserve of specific nations, though the best rock climbers still tend to come from Alpine nations – America, Japan and the European countries.

The level of confidence instilled by modern protection and techniques developed indoors has allowed phenomenal routes to be climbed. To stand beneath some of the top-graded climbs and look up is to be amazed not only at the ability, but at the sheer audacity of the climbers at the top of the sport. To define a 'best climb' is ludicrous as such things are a matter of opinion, but there are many who believe that the beautiful, improbable line of The Indian Face, climbed by Briton Johnny Dawes on the east buttress

of Snowdonia's Clogwyn d'Arddu in Wales, is, if not the hardest, then the finest rock climb in the world.

As with alpinism, the techniques acquired on the rock faces of Europe and America were soon transferred to the great ranges. Climbs on the spires of Patagonia – Fitzroy, Cerro Torre and the Paine group – are now of comparable difficulty. While these peaks are of similar height to those of the European Alps, the weather conditions are most certainly not, making hard climbing more than a matter of technique. In 1976 the British two-man team of Pete Boardman and Joe Tasker climbed Changabang's west face (sadly this brilliant pairing was to die trying to make the first ascent of Everest's north-east ridge), while in 1984 a Norwegian team climbed a new route on Great Trango Tower in the Karakoram – bringing modern standards of rock climbing to the highest peaks.

WOMEN AT THE SHARP END

It was once said that all climbs had a life which went through three phases. The initial phase included the first ascent and then the first few repeats during which time the climb's aura of difficulty was gradually reduced. In the second phase the climb would be accomplished by ordinary mortals. To give an example, the Eiger North Face's first party can be named by most climbers. The repeat ascents were by the famous climbers of the day, all eager to try themselves against the notorious wall. Terray and Lachenal, Buhl and Rebuffat, Bonington and Haston. Eventually the wall lost the air of invincibility which implied that only such masters could hope to succeed, and it was handed over to people unknown to the climbing world at large.

The third phase identified for a climb was 'easy day for a lady', a phrase which at once disparaged both the climb and female climbers. In the Golden Age such a view might have been sustainable. Etiquette required that women climbed in skirts, a mode of dress guaranteed to make the easiest climb hard. Some of the more adventurous women set off in the required form of dress, but stopped early to change into trousers or to remove their dress to reveal trousers underneath. Elizabeth Hawkins-Whitshed took her maid as high as the girl would go, to help her lace up her climbing boots. In 1838 the Comtesse Henriette d'Angeville climbed Mont Blanc dressed as a man: on the summit she sat on the shoulders of her guide and claimed to have climbed higher than any other human being. (The Comtesse was not the first woman to the summit, this having been a local woman, Maria Paradis, in 1808: it was her first and, it would seem, only climb.)

There were exceptions to the 'easy day' idea. Lucy Walker, the first woman to climb the Matterhorn, was one. Her father and uncle were climbers and employed the great Melchior Anderegg as guide. Lucy fell in love with him (a love which was never consummated: she died unmarried) and he helped her climb the Matterhorn to beat her rival, Meta Brevoort, in the race for first ascent by a woman. Miss Brevoort's guide

above

Hettie Dyhrenfurth, who was a member of her husband's 1930 expedition which attempted to climb Kangchenjunga.

was Christian Almer, the other great guide of the era who was himself in silent competition with Anderegg.

In 1888 a British newspaper accepted the presence of women in the Alps by suggesting in their notes on the Alpine season that the major honours for the year went to Katherine Richardson, a woman whose fragile frame hid a fierce determination. Another who fitted that description was the mysterious Lily Bristow, a schoolfriend of Albert Mummery's wife, who did many climbs with Mummery. Almost nothing is known of Lily – neither her birth date, nor when she died – except that her climbing career with Mummery was cut short, perhaps by Mrs Mummery's suspicions over her relationship with her husband.

Despite the efforts of these women, the Alpine Club declined to open its doors to them, causing Mrs Mummery to note caustically that it seemed their view was that a 'woman …should be satisfied with watching through a telescope …or by listening …(to the) sickening drawl (of) the many perils her returning husband had encountered. It was 100 years before the Club changed its mind. In other countries the clubs were less exclusive, though it was not until 1980 that Chamonix's Martine Rolland became the first official female Alpine guide.

By then women had made significant contributions to climbing. In 1934 Loulou Boulaz, climbing with Raymond Lambert, made an early attempt on the north face (Croz Spur) of the Grandes Jorasses: the pair were unsuccessful, but made an early repeat of the route when it was climbed a few weeks later. On the great ranges, a world altitude record was claimed by the American Annie Smith Peck who climbed the 5,699m (18,697 ft) Andean volcano Orizaba (now called Citlaltepetl) at the age of 47. In 1904 she raised the record to 5,800m (19,028 ft) on Illampu, another Andean peak, though she failed to reach the summit. She was now in competition with another American, Fanny Bullock-Workman who with her husband (and occasionally Matthias Zurbriggen) explored the Himalayas and Karakoram. Fanny, a committed feminist, climbed Pinnacle Peak in the Nun Kun region which was thought at the time (1907) to be over 7,000m (22,965 ft) , though it is now measured at 6,957m (22,824 ft). Annie Smith Peck retaliated by climbing the north peak of Huascaran in the Andes which, she said, was 7,300m (23,950 ft). She also claimed that the south peak, higher by 100m, was the highest summit in South America. An incensed Fanny sent an expedition, financed with her own money, to measure the height correctly: it was 6,650m (21,817 ft), and so her own record stood. Furthermore, the south peak was 6,763m (22,188 ft) and so Aconcagua was still the highest on the continent.

In the 1930s Hettie Dyhrenfurth also explored the Himalayas, with her husband Günther, though the next significant landmark was not until 1954 when Mme Claude Kogan was part of a Swiss team vying for the first ascent of Cho Oyu, the world's sixth-highest mountain. An Austrian team succeeded, the

below

Rebecca Stephens, the first British woman to climb Everest, and the first British woman (and third woman) to complete the Seven Summits.

above

The first three women to reach the summit of Everest. On the right, the Japanese Junko Tabei who was the first woman to do so on 16 May 1975, climbing from Nepal (she was also the first woman to climb the Seven Summits). In the centre, the Tibetan Phantog who reached the summit 11 days later from Tibet. To the left is Wanda Rutkiewicz who reached the summit in 1978. Rutkiewicz, who died on Kangchenjunga, still holds the record for female ascents of 8,000m peaks.

Swiss failing to notch up the second ascent. Mme Kogan died on Cho Oyu in 1959 when leading an all-women's expedition in an attempt to repeat the climb. Not until 1974 did a woman stand on the summit of an 8,000m (26,246 ft) peak when a Japanese team climbed Manaslu. The following year the Japanese Junko Tabei climbed Everest by the South Col route, beating by 11 days a Tibetan woman, Phantog, who climbed from the north side. That same year, the Polish woman Wanda Rutkiewicz led a team which climbed Gasherbrum III, 7,952m (26,089 ft), the highest peak to have had a first ascent by a woman. Rutkiewicz led a women's team up the Matterhorn's north face in winter in 1978, then set out to be the first woman to climb all fourteen 8,000m peaks. As this feat had been achieved only by a handful of men at the time, women were now competing at the pinnacle of the sport. Rutkiewicz climbed eight 8,000m peaks (including Everest, third female ascent, and K2, first female ascent) before disappearing on Kangchenjunga. In terms of 8,000m ascents, she is still the most successful high altitude woman climber. Rebecca Stephens became the first British woman to climb Everest in 1993 while in 1995 another Briton, Alison Hargreaves, became the first woman to have made a confirmed ascent of Everest without bottled oxygen (there having been a disputed climb in 1988).

At lower altitudes women are also now competing with men at the highest levels. Catherine Destivelle's ascent of a new route on the Dru has already been mentioned. The French woman also made the first repeat of Bonatti's Matterhorn north face route, solo and in winter. In Britain she soloed the Old Man of Hoy, not the country's hardest climb, but a very spectacular sea stack. Then, in 1993, American woman Lynn Hill achieved a climb which was coveted by, but had defeated, many top male climbers, making the first free (i.e. aid-less) ascent of the Nose on Yosemite's El Capitan.

THE GREAT RANGES

At the end of the 19th century — indeed, almost from the end of the Golden Age of Alpine climbing — climbers began to look further afield for unclimbed peaks. Freshfield headed towards the Caucasus. In Africa the German Ludwig Purtscheller climbed Kilimanjaro, while the Briton Harold Mackinder climbed Mount Kenya, in 1899, a climb which involved the bashing of a trail through primeval forest; this was not repeated for 30 years when another British team, including Eric Shipton and Wyn Harris, braved the same approach.

In New Zealand, attempts to climb Mount Cook began in 1882, but it was not until 1894, after numerous failures, that a team of young New Zealanders — Tom Fyfe, Jack Clarke and George Graham — reached the top by a route which was not to be repeated for more than 60 years. This local team had been spurred to make the ascent by the arrival of the experienced Briton Edward Fitzgerald and his guide, Matthias Zurbriggen. Fitzgerald was miffed by the locals' having made the climb and declined to make

right
An aerial photograph of Mount Cook from the south, over the Hooker Valley. Taken in winter, the shot shows the formidable nature of the peak. A few years ago a rock fall from the summit altered the height a little. Sadly it did not add to it — Mount Cook would have been a fine addition to the list of continental summits, a more worthy candidate than Kosciusko or even the Carstenz Pyramid.

Cerro Torre in Patagonia. The extreme nature of the climbing, together with the unpredictable and often atrocious weather, make it one of the world's most difficult peaks. Mystery still surrounds its first ascent which was hailed at the time as the finest climb of all time but is now viewed with suspicion by many experts.

a second ascent. Zurbriggen was less bothered and soloed a different, far easier route.

Fitzgerald and Zurbriggen moved on to South America, though they were following in the footsteps of Whymper who had already visited the continent, climbing Chimborazo in 1880. Fitzgerald and Zurbriggen wanted Aconcagua, the highest peak. In 1897 they succeeded, though again it was only Zurbriggen who reached the top. Much later, the high-angled ice slopes of the Andean peaks, and the sheer rock peaks of Patagonia were to attract the attention of the world's great climbers. In 1951 Lionel Terray led a team in the first ascent of Huantsan, while the same year also saw the first ascent of Alpamayo which many claim to be the most beautiful mountain the world. (The other main claimant for this title is Siniolchu in Sikkim, but everyone will have their own contender.) Terray was back in 1952, climbing Fitzroy, the highest of the Patagonian peaks, with Guido Magnone as part of a French team. Later Terray claimed that the climbing of Cerro Torre, next to Fitzroy, was the greatest mountaineering feat of all time. In fact it has also become the most controversial.

In 1959 a three-man team camped below the peak. One man soon abandoned the attempt, but the other two continued. One was Cesare Maestri, the leading Italian climber of his day, a master rock climber whose abilities and solo ascents were comparable with those of Hermann Buhl. The other was the Austrian Toni Egger. Days later Maestri returned alone, claiming to have reached the summit with Egger but to have descended alone after Egger was swept away by an avalanche. Inconsistencies in his account of the climb, and later attempts on the peak raised doubts as to the validity of Maestri's claim. Outraged by the doubters Maestri returned to Cerro Torre, using a 60kg (132 lb) compressed-air gun to slam bolts into the rock which he used to climb to the mushroom of ice which surmounts the summit. This he could not climb. It was now the turn of the rest of the climbing world to be outraged, especially as Maestri had left the compressor hanging from a bolt near the top of the peak. Subsequently Cerro Torre has been climbed several times, one climb over the line of Maestri's claimed first route merely adding to the initial doubts. However, Maestri has never changed his story and remains defiant.

THE HIGHEST PEAKS

For many the only great range is the Himalaya/Karakoram where the world's highest mountains are congregated. Exploration of these began with the surveyors of British India, several claims being made of heights reached during the last years of the 19th century. The first true expedition was that of Albert Mummery, the foremost British mountaineer of his era, a man who embraced the modern approach, climbing hard routes for the joy of doing it rather than to reach a summit. With two other pioneering Britons, Norman Collie and Geoffrey Hastings, and two Gurkhas, Mummery set off to climb Nanga Parbat in 1895. Mummery and the two Gurkhas disappeared after abandoning an attempt on the Diamir face, probably killed by an avalanche as they attempted to cross the Diamir Pass. In 1907 another Briton, Tom Longstaff, together with two French guides, the Brocherel brothers, reached the summit of Trisul (7,120m / 23,359 ft), surpassing Zurbriggen's ascent of Aconcagua as the highest summit to have been reached. This record was broken by the 1930 International Expedition (led by the Swiss Günther Dyhrenfurth) which climbed Jonsong (7,420m / 24,343 ft). The new record stood for just one year, until the British climbed Kamet (7,756m / 25,446 ft). Eric Shipton and Frank Smythe were among those who reached the top. The summit height record was increased again in 1936 when Bill Tilman and Noel Odell, members of an Anglo–American

below
The only known photograph of Albert Mummery climbing. It was taken by Lily Bristow, a noted woman climber whose partnership with Mummery ended abruptly, probably because Mummery's wife became nervous of the relationship.

far right
Dr Tom Longstaff. Longstaff was a qualified doctor, rich enough not to have to practise, who spent years exploring the Himalaya where 'his pirate beard blazed red against the Himalaya snows' according to one companion. Longstaff's climb of Trisul was the highest summit reached for over 20 years.

above

Holdsworth on the
summit of Kamet. As
with the other members
of the British team he is
only referred to by
surname throughout the
book on the expedition.
On the pre-climb photo,
Holdsworth has his pipe
clenched between his
teeth. On the summit it
is still there.

right

Nanda Devi from the
south. The mountain is
among the most
beautiful in the world. It
is also one of the most
difficult to approach,
requiring a difficult walk
through the Rishi Gorge
to reach an inner
sanctuary above which
the peak rises. This shot
was taken by Tilman
during the 1936
expedition.

team, reached the summit of Nanda Devi (7,816m / 25,643 ft). After the 1939–45 war, the French climbed
Annapurna (8,047m / 26,400 ft) in 1950, before the British claimed the highest peak of all in 1953.

In terms of height reached, the peak records from 1907 onwards were rendered irrelevant by the
early British expeditions to Everest. The first of these was in 1921, led by Charles Howard-Bury and
including George Mallory, whose name has become inextricably linked with the peak. Unable to go
through Nepal, at that time closed to outsiders, the British used their influence with Tibet to approach
the north side of the mountain. The team reached the North Col before being forced back by bad weather.
In 1922 the British returned, passing the 8,000m (26,246 ft) contour for the first time. George Finch and
Geoffrey Bruce finally reached a height of 8,320m (27,296 ft), but the expedition was marred by the death
of seven Sherpas in an avalanche. In 1924 the third expedition pushed the achieved height record to
8,570m (28,116 ft), Edward Norton reaching this height alone after his companion, Howard Somervell,
was forced to abandon his attempt due to high-altitude cough. But it is not for that record altitude that the
1924 expedition is remembered. A few days after Norton's attempt, a final climb was made by Mallory and

left

Mallory and Norton at their high point in 1922. Although the record for the highest peak attained increased steadily throughout the first half of the 20th century, finally going beyond 8,000 m for the first time in 1950 with the ascent of Annapurna, the heights reached by the Everest expeditions of the 1920s overtopped all summits except Everest itself. Mallory and Norton, together with Somervell, were the first to cross the 8,000 m contour, eventually reaching 8,200 m (26,900 ft). A few days later, Finch and Geoffrey Bruce reached 8,320 m (27,300 ft). Not only was this the highest point reached on the 1922 expedition, but it was also memorable as it was Bruce's first ever climb.

Sandy Irvine. The pair set out from the last camp on 8 June and were seen around midday by Noel Odell as he climbed up to support them. They were never again seen alive.

The finding of Mallory's body in 1999 answers one question that had been discussed ever since the disappearance and, more importantly, the discovery of Irvine's axe in 1933. Mallory still had a rope attached to his waist so the pair had definitely been climbing together when an accident occurred. It is conjectured from the site of the body that they were climbing down, something which accords with the position of the axe which was below the point at which Odell last saw the pair. The axe could have marked the point where an accident occurred, perhaps falling from Irvine's hand when he was startled by Mallory's fall. But these considerations do not answer the fundamental question – if the pair were indeed climbing down, as now seems indisputable, from where were they coming? Odell's sighting is crucial here, but over the years his opinion of where he saw the pair changed. At first he said it had been at or above the Second Step, the formidable obstacle that occupied the Chinese for several hours during the first known ascent of the north side of Everest. If Odell was correct then the summit might well have been reached. Later Odell changed his mind, believing his sighting was of the pair when they were much

right

Mallory and Irvine preparing to leave the North Col camp during the 1924 expedition. The oxygen equipment which they hoped would help them to the summit can be seen. This was the last photograph taken of the pair before they climbed into history. Ironically the shot was taken by Noel Odell who, a couple of days later, was the last man to see the pair alive. Had he taken another photograph then it would have helped solve the mystery of how far the two men climbed. Had a shot shown them below the Second Step then there would be few who would doubt their failure. Had one showed them above the Second Step (as Odell initially claimed) then it would have been tantalising evidence of success.

right

Unless Mallory and Irvine went higher, Norton's record from the 1924 expedition was to stand for almost 30 years. Leaving his climbing companion, Norton reached a height of about 8,550m (28,051 ft) before turning around when he realised that his rate of ascent was too slow for success.

above

A panoramic view of the north side of Everest from shots taken by Charles Howard-Bury on the 1921 expedition. The photos were taken from Lhakpa La (Windy Col or Windy Gap). To the right is Changste. Between it and Everest is the Chang La or North Col as the British called it. Running towards the camera from Everest is the North-East (Pinnacle) Ridge. From this vantage point the British could see that a route existed via the North Col and North-West Face. Just how much of the mountain is left to climb after the North Col has been reached is clear from this panorama.

right and opposite

In 1933 the British society hostess Lady Houston sponsored an expedition to fly over the summit of Everest. Two planes were used, both Westland PV3s, one renamed the Houston-Westland in the sponsor's honour. In the left-hand photo, one of the planes is being fuelled by hand pump and hosepipe, that and the clothing of both the British and local helpers saying as much about the era as photos of climbers in Norfolk jackets. In the photo opposite, the planes approach Everest. Because of downdraughts only exceptional pilot skills stopped the planes plunging into the mountain, the summit being cleared by only 150m (500 ft).

lower. In that case it is unlikely they had reached the top. There is a tantalising story of a Chinese climber spotting what could only have been Irvine's body, but searches to date have failed to locate it. Irvine is thought to have carried a camera, offering the possibility of a definitive answer to the mystery as film is preserved in the cold air (as it was for Andrée's Arctic balloon expedition). Unless or until that film is discovered, the mystery will remain.

After the loss of Mallory and Irvine the British were prevented by the Tibetans from returning to renew their efforts until 1933 (when Irvine's axe was found). On that trip Norton's height record was equalled (by Wyn Harris and Lawrence Wager climbing together and, later, by Frank Smythe climbing alone). An expedition in 1935 led by Eric Shipton included a young Sherpa called Tenzing Norgay. That, and other

attempts in 1936 and 1938, did not improve on the height record. The 1939–45 war ended attempts for a decade. By the 1950s, Tibet had closed its borders, while Nepal had opened up, allowing climbers to see that a much easier route could be forged on the southern side.

The Swiss attempted this in 1952, the north side height record being bettered by Raymond Lambert and Tenzing Norgay who reached 8,600m (28,215 ft) on the south-east ridge. It was this route that the successful British expedition of 1953 followed, the New Zealander, Edmund Hillary, and Tenzing reaching the summit on 29 May. Subsequently the summit has been reached by over 1,000 climbers, with, occasionally, dozens completing the climb on days of perfect weather.

Although many repeat the classic route – now disparagingly referred to as the Yak Route – climbers seeking a challenge on the world's highest peak have also searched out harder ways to the top. The Chinese pioneered the north ridge route, the Americans climbed the west ridge, and later the east face, the British the south-west face, the Australians the north face. A small Anglo–American team completed another route on the east face. The hardest routes are probably those forged by a Russian team (the south-west pillar) and a Polish team (south pillar). The summit has also been reached in winter. Most notably, after the mountain had been summited 60 or so times using bottled oxygen, the Italian Reinhold Messner

above

The Swiss Everest Expedition 1952. The Swiss attempted the peak twice in that year, pre- and post-monsoon. In the spring they placed a camp at 8,400m (27,559 ft). The photo shows the Swiss climbers Flory and Aubert flanking Tenzing Norgay. The two Swiss had helped Tenzing and Raymond Lambert carry to this point on the South-East Ridge where the last camp was established. The next day Lambert and Tenzing reached 8,600m (28,215 ft), but were defeated by bad weather and the sheer effort of climbing in the thin air, despite their use of bottled oxygen. The peak in the background is Makalu, the world's fifth-highest mountain.

and Austrian Peter Habeler climbed Everest without it, a feat repeated many times since. Messner also climbed the mountain solo and without bottled gas, choosing the monsoon season as the peak is somewhat crowded at other times. This climb, from the north side, was the pinnacle of Messner's remarkable career as a climber. Equally noteworthy is the achievement of the Sherpa Ang Rita, who has reached the top ten times.

THE 8,000M PEAKS

Everest is one of 14 mountains which rise above the 8,000m (26,250 ft) contour. The history of climbing on those peaks mirrors that of the Golden Age of alpinism. At first, climbers were interested in reaching the tops. Then, with the peaks climbed, they turned their attentions to harder routes on the 14 as well as harder routes on lower peaks. The first of the 14 to be climbed was Annapurna in 1950, just after Nepal had opened its borders to foreigners. The French team that went to Annapurna was one of the strongest ever assembled, Lionel Terray, Louis Lachenal and Gaston Rebuffat being among the best climbers in the world at the time, having learned their trade during the Alpine resistance movement of the 1939–45 war. Annapurna was climbed by Lachenal and expedition leader Maurice Herzog, but the remarkable success

right

Charles Evans on the
South Summit of Everest
after its first ascent. The
photograph was taken by
Tom Bourdillon who then
descended towards the
col between the South
Summit and the final
ridge. Though in the
official version of events
the two climbers were
content to return from the
South Summit, it is said
that Bourdillon always
wished he had pushed on
towards the main summit.

right
Three days after Bourdillon and Evans reached the South
Summit, Hillary and Tenzing became the first men to
stand on top of the world. Hillary took several photos of
Tenzing, one of them becoming a mountaineering icon.
There is no photo of Hillary on the summit.

of the expedition was marred by its aftermath,
the two men being trapped high on the mountain
and succumbing to terrible frostbite injuries.
Herzog lost his fingers and toes (and was lucky to
survive at all), Lachenal lost his toes. Herzog
never climbed seriously again. For Lachenal, a
professional guide, the loss of his toes was a
disaster. He never regained his former brilliance
and died in a skiing accident.

Everest was the next 8,000m to be climbed,
followed by success on Nanga Parbat, also in
1953. Nanga Parbat has a tragic history, almost all
of it involving German expeditions. In 1930 an
expedition under Willy Merkl, including Willo
Welzenbach and Fritz Wiessner, as well as Rand
Herron, an American, explored a long route up the
face of the Rakhiot Peak, aiming to cross the Silver
Saddle and Silver Plateau to reach Nanga Parbat's
northern ridge. The team reached about 7,000m
(22,965 ft), where bad weather and inexperience
stopped them. Stopping over at Cairo on the
return, Rand Herron was killed when he fell
descending the Great Pyramid.

In 1934 the Germans returned, again under
Merkl, with Welzenbach also in the team. This
time they reached the Silver Saddle but were
caught in a violent storm. Attempting to retreat,
Merkl, Welzenbach and a third German, Uli
Wieland, died together with six Sherpas in a tale
of drawn-out agony, the men dying in their tracks
as they hauled themselves, frostbitten and
exhausted, down the mountain.

The tragedy was a blow to German pride, one
which they immediately sought to rectify. But
worse was to follow: in 1937 virtually the entire
team was overwhelmed in their sleep when a
huge avalanche struck their camp. Sixteen men
died instantly. In 1938 a new attempt failed,
fortunately with no loss of life. The Germans tried

Maurice Herzog on the summit of Annapurna, the first 8000m peak to be climbed. The snow slope to the right caused some to question the climb, as it appears that there is a lot more mountain still above the triumphant climber. The photograph was one of several taken by Herzog's companion Louis Lachenal, the others showing much less of a slope. The summit was corniced so that Herzog had to stand a little way from the edge to avoid a fall. That, and the fact that Lachenal is well below him, looking up, explains the apparent anomaly.

right

Uli Wieland making his way towards the Moor's Head (the prominent rock pillar) during the 1934 German Nanga Parbat expedition. Above Wieland are the twin peaks of the Silver Saddle, beyond which the Silver Plateau leads to the summit. The storm which killed many members of the team blew up while the Germans were on the Plateau, the climbers dying during the agonising descent from the Silver Saddle.

opposite

Hermann Buhl's ice axe in the summit snow of Nanga Parbat. The flag is framed by the twin peaks of the Silver Saddle. Buhl's solo climb to the summit is still considered by many to be the most remarkable in the history of high-altitude climbing. Buhl left his ice axe on the summit, though it was not found until 1995 when a Japanese team climbed Nanga Parbat along a new route which included a section of Buhl's final summit climb. They found the axe and returned it to his wife.

again in 1939, determined to climb what was now becoming seen as a German peak, so much so that a British suggestion that they might try Nanga Parbat was greeted with indignation in Germany. The 1939 expedition was interned in British India when war was declared, one of its members, Heinrich Harrer, who had climbed the Eiger North Face the year before, escaping into Tibet, a journey which he recounted in *Seven Years in Tibet*.

The death toll increased again in 1950 when three young Britons, accompanied by several Sherpas including Tenzing Norgay, camped below Nanga Parbat. They were poorly equipped for winter climbing, but against the advice of Tenzing they attacked the mountain. One soon retreated with frostbite, but the other two continued. They were never seen again. Three years later, as the British were climbing Everest, another German team arrived, one which included a single Austrian, Hermann Buhl, arguably the greatest climber of the day. The Germans followed the route of the pre-war expeditions, but delays due to spurious decisions by the non-climbing leader meant that the intended top camps were not established. As a result the final attempt – by Buhl and another climber – started very low. Buhl's companion stopped early, but Buhl continued alone. In a climb which for triumph of will has never been

above

One of a series of panoramic shots taken by Vittorio Sella during the Karakoram expedition led by the Duke of the Abruzzi in 1909. Sella, nephew of the man who founded the Italian Alpine Club, is now recognised as one of the greatest – perhaps the greatest – mountain photographer. This shot is a section of a panorama of the Baltoro Glacier. In the distance to the left is K2, the world's second highest mountain. In the centre is the massive bulk of Broad Peak, its three summits clearly visible. To the right is Gasherbrum IV. The ascent of the face of the latter peak which is towards the camera is claimed by many to be the greatest high altitude climb accomplished to date.

equalled he reached the summit after toiling upwards for 16½ hours. Caught out by nightfall on the way down he spent the long hours of darkness standing on a small ledge, continuing his downward climb at dawn. Finally, after 40½ hours alone, he reached the top camp. Despite being severely dehydrated Buhl survived, though he did lose toes to frostbite.

Next to fall was K2, the second highest mountain in the world and, by common consent, the hardest. It had first been visited as early as 1909 by an Italian team which included Vittorio Sella who some still regard as the best of all mountain photographers. That expedition made only a cursory attempt of the peak (though it identified the best route to the top, now called the Abruzzi Ridge after the Duke of the Abruzzi who led the expedition). The first concerted attempt waited until 1938, when an American team solved the problem of the lower part of the ridge, only to be defeated by bad weather. Americans returned in 1939, a different team, led by Fritz Wiessner who had been on Nanga Parbat with the Germans in 1930 but was now a naturalised American. Wiessner and the Sherpa Pasang Dawa Lama almost reached the top (getting to within 240m / 787 ft) and probably would have reached it had Wiessner not chosen the more difficult of two possible routes on the last day. But this magnificent achievement was overshadowed by the death of one American and three Sherpas, deaths which resulted in accusations against Wiessner, counter-accusations and general unpleasantness.

In the aftermath of the 1939–45 war the Americans tried again; in 1953, Charles Houston's team were forced to retreat by bad weather and the illness of one team member. In a tragic accident this man, Art Gilkey, was swept to his death as he lay helpless on a stretcher after those rescuing him had had to leave him for a few minutes to save themselves. Finally, in 1954, a large Italian team succeeded in climbing K2. The team included Walter Bonatti, the leading Italian alpinist of the era. He did not reach the

left
The ridge camp at about 6,000m (19,685 ft) during one of
the German attempts to climb Kangchenjunga along its
North-East Spur in the 1930s. The Spur was not climbed
until 1977 when an Indian Army expedition succeeded in
following it to the North Ridge and on to the summit.

top, but his selfless climb, to bring oxygen bottles to the two who did, assured them of victory.

Cho Oyu, the world's sixth-highest mountain and, by common consent, one of the easiest 8,000m peaks, was also climbed in 1954 by a small team of Austrians. Makalu (French, 1955), Kangchenjunga (British, 1955), Manaslu (Japanese, 1956) and Lhotse (Swiss, 1956 – the expedition also made the second ascent of Everest) were all climbed by large national expeditions, the next forward step in high-altitude climbing being made in summer 1956, when Gasherbrum II was climbed by an Austrian team. Although this expedition followed established methods – porters stocking a line of camps – it differed in deliberately bivouacing on the summit climb, an alpine technique not used before (though Buhl had been forced to bivouac on Nanga Parbat).

Large, national expeditions were also used on the first ascents of the last three 8,000m peaks,

opposite

Marcus Schmuck on the summit of Broad Peak after the
first ascent. The photo was taken by Fritz Wintersteller.
Broad Peak was climbed by a four man team without
using porters, a huge advance in technique for high
altitude climbing. Behind Schmuck is K2. As on
Annapurna, the summit was found to be heavily corniced
so Schmuck has stopped a few steps short to avoid
collapsing the cornice and falling to his death. Ironically,
Hermann Buhl, who reached the summit later the same
day, was killed when a cornice collapsed on Chogolisa a
few days after the successful Broad Peak climb. With
commercial expeditions to many 8000m peaks now
available, climbs of Broad Peak are relatively common:
the peak was not climbed for 20 years after the first
ascent, but over 200 climbers had reached the top by the
end of the century. Some climbs are controversial. On the
first ascent the Austrians climbed what they thought was
the summit, but later discovered it was a 'forepeak' the
main summit, not much higher, being a further hour's
climbing along a ridge. Many climbers reach only the
forepeak, but claim a real ascent.

right

Joe Brown at the summit of Kangchenjunga after the first
ascent. The book of the climb is called *The Untrodden
Peak* as the British expedition which completed the climb
gave an undertaking to local people that the summit,
which they believed to be the home of their gods, would
remain undisturbed. The final summit snows can be seen
behind Brown. At first, subsequent climbers also left the
summit untrodden, but recent photos suggest that the
climbers are ignoring the original vow.

Joe Brown was accompanied to Kangchenjunga's
summit by George Band. In Britain, Brown, at first climbing
with Don Whillans, made a dramatic improvement in the
standard of rock climbing and remained the major figure in
the sport for about 20 years, a remarkable achievement.

Gasherbrum I (American, 1958), Dhaulagiri (Swiss/Austrian, 1960) and Shisha
Pangma (Chinese, 1964). The very notable exception was the ascent of Broad
Peak in 1957 by a four-man Austrian team climbing without porters. The team,
leader Marcus Schmuck, Fritz Wintersteller, Hermann Buhl and Kurt Diemberger,
established three camps, then climbed over the mountain's forepeak to the
main summit. (Itself 8,000m and the scene of many an abandoned climb,
many of those that stop on the forepeak claim to have climbed the mountain.)
Schmuck and Wintersteller reached the main summit ahead of Buhl, who
was suffering with a stomach upset, and Diemberger. Hermann Buhl thus
became the first man to the top of two 8,000m peaks. The only other man to
achieve this is Kurt Diemberger who was also on the first climb of Dhaulagiri.
(The Sherpa Gyalzen is considered by some to be a member of this most
exclusive club, having reached the top of Makalu on 16 May, after Lionel
Terray and Jean Couzy had climbed the peak for the first time on 15 May, and
then to have been on the first ascent of Manaslu.)

The 8,000m peaks were climbed between 1950 and 1964, almost exactly the
same length of time as the Golden Age of alpine climbing. As with the Alps, these
climbs had generally been along ridges: in the next phase Himalayan climbers
moved to the faces which were steeper, the climbing more difficult, just as
they had in the Alps. On these faces the most important climbs were in 1970

when a British team led by Chris (now Sir Chris) Bonington climbed the awesome south face of Annapurna and a German team climbed Nanga Parbat's Rupal Face, claimed to be the highest mountain face in the world. Later, many of Bonington's team returned to the Himalaya with him to climb Everest's south-west face. Other faces were also climbed, at first by large teams, then by smaller ones.

The ultimate – though such things are, of course, a matter of opinion – were the solo climbs of the Slovenians, Tomo Cesen up the south face of Lhotse, and Tomaz Humar, up the south face of Dhaulagiri. Unfortunately Cesen's ascent has been questioned, casting a shadow over it. Humar did not reach the summit of Dhaulagiri (but admitted as much). This might have been seen as the first climb of a new phase of high-altitude climbing when, as in the Alps, it became unnecessary to reach the summit for a successful climb of a new route. But this was not the case: Humar wanted the summit, as everyone does on an 8,000m peak, but was forced to retreat by sheer exhaustion after completing the face.

Though climbing harder routes on the 8,000m peaks was the ambition of many climbers, many more simply wished to reach the summits of one or several. Inevitably climbers wanted to climb all 14, though the first man to achieve this feat, the Italian Reinhold Messner, claimed it had not been his intention at the start of his 8,000m career. Soon after Messner succeeded, the Pole Jerzy Kukucka became the second man to complete the set. By the end of 1999 the number who had done so had increased to six. At the time of writing (with some expeditions still in progress) it is quite likely to have reached double figures.

THE SEVEN SUMMITS

In 1985 the American Dick Bass claimed victory in the 'race' to become the first person to have stood on the summits of all seven continents. It was a notable achievement, but one which was immediately controversial.

The first controversy was whether Bass (and others involved in the 'race') had been correct in defining seven continents. The argument in favour of seven involves plate tectonics, the movement of the vast plates on which the land surfaces of the earth ride, the collision of which give rise to such diverse phenomena as the volcanoes in Iceland and the Himalayas. In general it is agreed that seven is an appropriate number, these being Europe, Asia, Africa, Antarctica, North America, South America and Australia. The division of America into north and south is accepted by almost everyone, but what exactly constitutes 'Australia' is quite a different matter. A second bone of contention is where exactly Europe ends as the traveller heads east from Portugal.

EVEREST

No one disputes that Everest is the highest peak in Asia. Its attainment is the ultimate problem for would-be seven summiters as it is in a different league to the other peaks. Everest is not a hard climb, unless one of the modern routes is taken, but because of the extreme vulnerability of summitters to weather and illness as a result of the thin air, it is a major undertaking. Human life cannot survive at 8,000m: all who climb above that height, even with bottled oxygen, are dying. The time to death varies with actual height and the individual, but in most people it is measured in hours, which makes rapid ascent and descent a necessity. Unfortunately, the nature of high-altitude climbing, even with bottled gas, makes rapid climbing, up or down, an impossibility.

above

Dick Bass on the summit of Everest. Bass, a corporate executive who owned the Snowbird ski resort in Utah and had other business interests, was able to finance his own expeditions. This fact, together with his not being a 'real' climber did not endear him to those professional mountaineers who were also trying to gain the Seven Summits, but who had to rely on sponsorship. Using his financial muscle, Bass won the race, but his decision to choose Kosciusko, the high point of Australia, allowed others to widen the continent to Australasia and so include the higher Carstenz Pyramid.

The formidable South
Face of Aconcagua
viewed from the
Horcones Valley. The
valley curves around the
western flank of the
peak and is followed by
the 'standard' route
which then ascends the
north-west/north side.
The South Face was
climbed by a French
team led by Réné Ferlet
in 1954, the climb
requiring six camps on
the face. The face is
both difficult and very
dangerous and is rarely
climbed.

ACONCAGUA

The highest peak in South America is, at 6,960m (22,835 ft), also the second highest of the seven summits. It was first climbed in 1896 when Edward Fitzgerald led a team that included Matthias Zurbriggen, the famous alpine guide. The team climbed the now-standard route – from the Horcones Valley and up the western side of the peak – but the summit was reached by Zurbriggen alone when the rest of the party were laid low with altitude problems. Later other members of the team did reach the summit, but sadly Fitzgerald was not one of them.

In 1934 a Polish team explored the eastern side of the mountain, making a route up what is now called the Polish Glacier. In the 1950s the mountain's south face, a vast expanse of ice and rock, attracted the attention of many of the world's best climbers. It was finally climbed by a French team in 1954. A variation on this route was climbed in 1974 by Reinhold Messner.

Today the mountain has as many as 1,500 ascents each year, though as many climbers again succumb to bad weather – the mountain is notorious for the *viento blanco*, the white wind, which reduces visibility and threatens to blow all and everything off the hill – or altitude problems.

McKINLEY

Though the National Park which now surrounds North America's highest peak (6,194m / 20,321 ft) has

right and below

Mount McKinley, the highest peak in North America. The peak stands in the Denali National Park in central Alaska. The upper photograph was taken from the Eielson Visitor Centre. The Centre (named for one of Alaska's most famous bush pilots) lies on the road which penetrates deep into the Park. Visitors cannot drive along it, but must take the Park bus. From the Centre the mountain rears above the Muldrow Glacier and shows the double summit structure distinctly. The right-hand (north) summit is that climbed (or claimed) by the 'Sourdough' expedition of 1910. The left-hand (south) summit – the true summit – was climbed in 1913.

In the lower photograph, sunset lights up McKinley's northern face. The shot was taken from Wonder Lake, the most remote camp site in the Denali National Park, one with limited sites which must be booked weeks in advance during the summer months. The camper is at the heart of the Park, with outstanding views of the mountain, but is tormented by millions of mosquitoes.

been renamed Denali, the native American name, meaning Great One, the peak itself is still usually called McKinley, after the twenty-fifth US President. The early history of the mountain is tied up with Dr Frederick Cook, the polar explorer who not only claimed to have made the first ascent, but also to have reached the North Pole the year before Peary's alleged journey. Cook first made an attempt on the peak in 1903, attempting to climb it from the north, but being defeated by the difficulties of the climb. Later the same year Cook led a party around the peak, a remarkable achievement, though the book written about the trip by one member of his team was less than flattering about the leader. Cook was committed to climbing McKinley, in part for commercial reasons as he had an advance from *Harper's Magazine* for the story of the climb. He therefore returned in 1906 with a new team, going up the Ruth Glacier to attempt the east buttress. Eventually the team was reduced to just two, Cook and Ed Barrill, who after three weeks returned with the stunning news that they had climbed the peak.

The claim was accepted at first, but doubts soon began, chiefly involving the times claimed for the climb, which seemed much too short for so arduous an ascent. Ultimately Barrill admitted that Cook had given him money to agree with the story and it was later shown that the photograph Cook claimed was taken at the summit was taken on a much lower peak many miles from McKinley. That said, it must be remembered that the controversy is not over, some still believing that Cook did indeed climb the route he claimed. It has been pointed out that Barrill was actually given cash after he had changed his story: so was he bribed to say yes or to say no, or to say both things at appropriate moments? In general the climbing world discounts Cook's claim, but as with his north pole trip it is not straightforward (though the latter is rather more credible as Cook's credentials as a polar explorer are quite clear).

right
Ludwig Purtscheller who
guided Hans Meyer to
the top of Kilimanjaro on
the first ascent.

Desert

Exploration of the great deserts of the world began very early, motivated by politics, the desire to map and understand these regions, or out of simple curiosity. Their geography, religion and politics were at times huge barriers to overcome – Richard Burton's entry into Mecca disguised as a pilgrim is one famous example. Their exploration continued into the 20th century, with Wilfred Thesiger being one of the most memorable and famous of the last 'true' explorers.

From the 7th century BC, Greek colonies pushed outwards north from the Aegean, undertaking expeditions as far as Georgia and Russia. Perhaps the most famous Greek 'explorer' was Alexander the Great. During an 11-year military campaign from 336 BC, he marched 20,000 miles through modern Turkey, Gaza, Egypt, Libya, Persia, Afghanistan and India and founded 70 cities.

A century after Alexander the Great's campaign, the Romans' love of silk contributed greatly to the foundation of the Silk Road. However, the route was not a medium solely for the interchange of goods, but of ideas too. During the first few centuries AD, the Silk Road was used in both directions for missionary journeys, by both Buddhists and Christians. It was the main route of exploration in this region until around the 16th century AD, after which time trade declined with the introduction of sea routes between Europe and Asia. The bustling cities of the Silk Road became submerged in the desert, only to be uncovered by explorers such as Marc Aurel Stein centuries later.

The rise of Islam and its 'golden age' between the 8th and 10th centuries AD brought great commercial prosperity, great scientific discoveries, and renewed curiosity amongst travellers to map and understand all the regions which made up the new Islamic world. One of the most famous names in Arabic exploration is that of Ibn Battuta, a lawyer born in Tangier in 1304. Following a journey to undertake the obligatory *hajj* – a pilgrimage to Mecca – Battuta decided to carry on travelling and continued for most of his life. He is thought to have covered over 75,000 miles in his exploration, taking in Cairo, Damascus, Alexandria, Tanzania, Persia, the Black, Caspian and Aral Seas, the Hindu Kush, India, South-East Asia and China, and finally to Granada, Tangier and across the Sahara. His account of these journeys, *The Travels*, contains much important geographical and cultural information.

The upper slopes of the
north-eastern side of
Kosciusko, taken from
just below the summit. A
lone skier can be seen in
the centre of the picture,
just below the skyline
ridge.

The irony of Pat Morrow's attempt to be the first man to complete the seven summits, and with Carstenz instead of Kosciusko, is that he was beaten by the American Gerry Roach who climbed both Kosciusko and Carstenz to be sure. Morrow also climbed both to become the third 'seven summiter'. In 1991, six years after Dick Bass, Junko Tabei, the first woman to climb Everest, became the first woman seven summiter. Frenchwoman Christine Janin became the first European woman to complete the set, with Rebecca Stephens the first British woman. Keith Kerr had by then become the first Briton to join a club which still boasts only some 100 members. As the list of members increases there are attempts to be the youngest or oldest member, and to complete the seven in the shortest possible time. In early 2001 the Briton Andrew Salter completed the set in 288 days. It is tempting to suggest that this time will take some beating, but the history of climbing is littered with such statements, almost all of which have returned to haunt those who made them.

An evening view of Kibo, Kilimanjaro's highest point, from the south-west. The photograph was taken from high in the forest of giant heather which clothes the upper reaches of the the Umbwe Ridge, the usual way to the Western Breach. This gap in the crater wall, which offers an interesting scrambling route to the top for those in the know, is obscured behind the branches on far left. The Great Breach Wall — occasionally known as the 'Eiger of Africa' — is left of centre. To the right of centre are the peak's southern glaciers — notably the Heim and the Kersten — which provide high standard mountaineering routes.

The next claim on the peak also has its doubters. In 1910 a team of four 'sourdoughs' — as gold prospectors in the area were known — accepted a bet to climb the peak and claimed to have reached what they discovered was the lower, north, summit. There they erected a spruce pole which they had carried up. The route they took has since frightened off a number of good climbers and the idea of climbing it with a pole seems far-fetched to many. The pole is said to have been seen when the true (south) summit was reached in 1913, but there are reasons to wonder if it really was. What is beyond doubt is that the team of Walter Harper, Harry Karstens, Hudson Stuck and Robert Tatum did indeed reach the highest point, an achievement which was not repeated for 30 years. Today there are numerous routes on the peak, including some very serious ones on the south face (the Cassin, named for Riccardo Cassin, the Italian who led the first successful climb in 1961, and the Scott/Haston route climbed by the first two men to ascend Everest's south-west face). The mountain has also been climbed in winter, a major undertaking as it lies so far north (at the edge of the Arctic Circle). On the first winter ascent the team had to contend with very low temperatures and high winds. The book of the climb is called *Minus 148°*, which gives the flavour. That temperature (in °F) equates to minus 100°C, and with wind speeds reaching 240kph (150mph) the wind chill is barely imaginable.

KILIMANJARO

Offering the vision of snow on the equator (well, near it, the peak lies 400kms/ 248 miles south of the line) and the even more astonishing view of elephants in front of a mountain that reaches almost 20,000ft (it is 5,895m – 19,340ft), Kilimanjaro is the easiest of the seven summits (with, perhaps, one exception – see Kosciusko, below). In 1887 the British missionary Charles New became the first person to reach the snowline, but went no higher, the first ascent following two years later when the German Hans Meyer climbed 'Kaiser Wilhelm Spitze' with his Swiss guide Ludwig Purtscheller. Today the highest top has been renamed Uhuru Peak (apparently the *Star Trek* lieutenant was named for the peak rather than the other way round). By one of the standard routes Kilimanjaro is little more than a trek as the weather is rarely a problem. What is a problem is the altitude which catches many unawares, especially if they do not acclim- atise properly beforehand. The peak also has some more demanding routes, the direct route on the Breach Wall giving Reinhold Messner what he claims was one of the most dangerous climbs of his life. He climbed the route's 1,500m (4,921 ft) in just 12 hours, a remarkable ascent rate.

ELBRUS

Most people, if asked for the highest mountain in Europe, would unhesitatingly answer 'Mont Blanc'. But if the dividing line between Europe and Asia is taken as the Urals, then the Caucasus lie in Europe and the 5,642m (18,510 ft) Elbrus overtops Mont Blanc by some 835m (2,739 ft). In Russia the first ascent of the lower, eastern, summit is credited to members of the Russian military and geographical expedition in 1829. It is said that a local man, Kilar Khashirov, acting as a guide, reached the summit alone after his equally fit companion, Akhya Sotaev, turned back to escort down a third member of the team who was sick. In the west this reasonably well-attested climb has been dismissed as fanciful, the reasons seemingly having more to do with prejudice than reality. The Sourdough ascent of McKinley – a much harder climb on a much higher mountain – is acclaimed as a triumph, while the equivalent climb by Russian sourdoughs is scoffed at. The unprejudiced view must be that Khashirov did indeed climb the lower summit in 1829.

At the time of his climb almost to the summit in 1829, Sotaev was 41. In 1868 he was 80 when he guided Douglas Freshfield's expedition to the eastern summit. Quite why the British, who had weather good enough to admire the view all round, did not climb the higher, west, summit is not clear. That summit was finally reached in 1874 by another British expedition. They were accompanied by the Swiss guide Peter Knubel. Knubel wanted a local man to help with the approach and was recommended Akhya Sotaev. The 86-year-old led them to the top, becoming the first man to reach both summits (and, probably, the oldest to reach either). The dome-shaped Elbrus offers little scope for new routes, though doubtless Russian climbers have done rather more than is known. For today's seven summiters, the standard route is much like the ascent of Kilimanjaro, a trek with snow towards the top and, again, the chief problem is altitude.

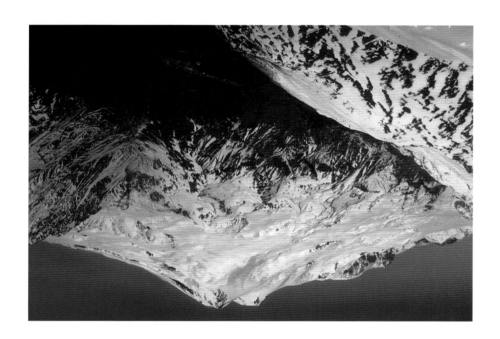

VINSON

Until 1957 the highest peak in Antarctica (at 4,897m / 16,066 ft) was undiscovered. In that year it was first seen from the air, though it was not until the area had been surveyed that it was realised that it was indeed the highest. It was then named, by the Americans, for Senator Carl Vinson who had done much to persuade the US government to support Antarctic exploration. It was climbed, in 1966, by the first team to attempt it, Pete Schoening (who had also been in the first party to climb Gasherbrum I), Barry Corbett, John Evans and Bill Long. Most climbers follow the route of the first ascent, but several other routes exist — most notable, one forged by a Slovenian team. The climbing is straightforward, but the local climate is, unsurprisingly, both cold and windswept. Rather more of a problem for aspirant seven summiters is extreme cost, Antarctica being a very expensive place to reach. With access strictly controlled, aspiring climbers are forced into one of a small number of travel possibilities, each of which involves serious expense.

right
Mount Vinson viewed from Mount Shinn top the south. The standard route starts from the bottom right of the photograph, following the ridge and then then plateau edge to the summit.

CARSTENZ, OR KOSCIUSKO

When Dick Bass completed his seven summits in 1985 his list included Mount Kosciusko (2,228m / 7,309 ft) in Australia, a peak named for a Polish hero, after the man who had made the first known ascent, Sir Paul Strzelecki, noted the similarity between its shape and that of the tomb of Tadeusz Kosciusko in Cracow Cathedral. It is very likely that Aborigines had reached the summit earlier, perhaps centuries earlier. Kosciusko's summit has been reached by bicycle, that fact alone probably prejudicing the climbing world against it. This led Pat Morrow, a Canadian who had been in quiet competition with Bass for the seven summits, to look for a more fitting choice. With support from geographers, Morrow extended the Australian continent to include adjacent islands

below

The Carstenz Pyramid.
The standard route to the
top is a rock climb up the
water-worn, but excellent
limestone of the peak's
north face. The exotic
position of the peak add to
the joys of the climb, but
the expense of reaching
such a remote area mean
that Carstenz is unlikely
to become a popular
destination for climbers
who are not seeking the
Seven Summits.

(Australasia or Oceania) and as a result saw the Carstenz Pyramid on West Papua (formerly Irian Jaya) as the seventh peak. Though claimed to have been seen by the Dutchman Jan Carstenz in about 1623, the peak was not actually proved to exist until the early 20th century when a British expedition hacked a way through the jungle to its base. A Dutch geographical expedition failed to climb the peak in 1936 and it was then left alone until 1961 when a further attempt failed. In the following year Heinrich Harrer, veteran of the Eiger north face, succeeded in leading a team to the top along what is now the standard route. Reinhold Messner added another route on the second ascent, while later climbers have made several more on the peak's north face. For climbers the expense of reaching West Papua is offset both by the climbing and by the chance to visit the people of the Dani tribe. Harrer's book on his expedition was called I Come from the Stone Age, a title which correctly reflected the Dani. It is not much changed today: Dani men still wear the koteka or penis gourd (and little else besides) despite the strenuous efforts of the authorities during Operation Koteka to impose a 'more 'modern' form of dress. It is claimed that when the first consignment of shorts were airlifted in at the start of the campaign the bemused Dani wore them as hats.

Prior to his adventures in Africa, Sir Richard Francis Burton had worked as an undercover intelligence officer in India and entered Mecca disguised as a *hajji*, a crime punishable by death. For the journey he even had himself circumcised. He followed this by becoming the first white man to enter the forbidden city of Harar in Somalia and leave alive. Burton's travels continued throughout the rest of his life, taking in Iceland, the Americas and Europe. His fascination with the Orient and human behaviour led him to be a master of its languages and he translated several Eastern texts, including the first unabridged translation of *Arabian Nights,* the *Kama Sutra* and *The Perfumed Garden*; translations of Italian, Roman and Persian poetry; and various popular texts with descriptions of tribal and sexual customs. He learnt to sidestep Victorian obscenity laws by publishing many of his works privately or abroad.

CENTRAL ASIA

The 'Great Game' begins the story of exploration in central Asia during the age of photography. This 'Game' (1800–1917) was a titanic, if covert, struggle between Russia and Britain. At stake was mastery of Central Asia and control of the vast Eurasian heartland and the mountain passes that led to India whose cotton, grain and other resources fuelled Britain's global empire. The outcome was thought by many to be the key to who would dominate world affairs for years to come. Halford Mackinder, the British founder of geopolitical theory, called the region the 'heartland of history' and claimed, 'he who controls Central Asia controls the world'. Played out during much of the 19th century, each imperial power attempted to carve out 'buffer states' as a protection against each other. Tsarist Russia was intent on expanding her borders south while the British Raj was just as determined that Peter the Great would not reach 'the warm waters of the Indian Ocean'.

The Great Trigonometrical Survey of India played a part in this 'game'. Launched in 1802, it aimed to map the Indian empire in its entirety, including the 3,000-kilometre (1,900-mile) arc of Himalayan mountains to its north. According to Matthew Edney in *Mapping an Empire: The Geographical Construction of British India, 1765–1843*, 'Map making was integral to British imperialism in India. The surveys and maps together transformed the subcontinent from an exotic and largely unknown region into a well-defined and knowable geographical entity. The empire might have defied the map's extent, but mapping defined the empire's nature.'

Not only did the Survey define and place Britain's existing Empire, it also aimed to serve as a tool for Britain's goal of extending beyond it. Of particular interest was Tibet, as this region beyond the Himalayas was virtually unexplored. British interest in Tibet was based not only on curiosity, but the desire to know what influence China had there, and what trade could be established. Later, growing Russian influence in the region would further drive British interest. However, mapping the geographically difficult and dangerous mountains and Tibet beyond them required men to be not only capable in surveying, but also in subterfuge and exploration.

Britain's first emissary, George Bogle, travelled to Tibet in 1774, forging links with the Panchen Lama, but failing to sign a trade agreement. He was followed by Lieutenant Samuel Turner, who attended the ceremony of the incarnation of the new Panchen Lama in 1783, thus paving the way for strong and profitable relations with the Tibetans. But in 1792, the intervention of the Nepalese and the tactical negligence of the East India's Governor General, Charles Cornwallis, was to prevent this relationship from developing. Cornwallis turned down a request from the Panchen Lama's Regent for help in defending Tibet against an advancing Nepalese army. As a result, Tibet felt compelled to turn to China for support, who repelled the Nepalese and encouraged the closure of the borders with Nepal and India to all but local traders and pilgrims.

With the gates to Tibet officially closed to Europeans, and the British in particular, there were several attempts by Europeans to enter Tibet in disguise, most notably the expedition of Thomas Manning and the expedition of Evarist Huc and Joseph Gabet, all of whom were discovered by the Tibetans and forced to leave in a matter of months. It was for this reason that, in the 1860s, Captain Montgomerie, a surveyor of the Trigonometrical Survey, decided to employ local people to provide them with geographical and political information of this forbidden land. By this stage, most of the region south and west of Tibet had been surveyed, and Mount Everest's height – named after another surveyor – had been calculated; Tibet remained a blank spot on an ever more-detailed map.

As native people would obviously be able to travel through Tibet much more freely, Montgomerie hired so-called 'pundits', who were trained for up to a year in surveying, navigation and 'spying' techniques. They learnt to walk with a measured stride, accurately recording the distances they travelled, using prayer beads as counting markers. To lessen the need for note-taking, they were also taught to memorise a huge amount of information by transcribing it into verse and chanting it like Buddhist prayers. They carried out their surveys using instruments such as compasses, sextants and thermometers hidden within their belongings.

Each of these clandestine traders or pilgrims had a code name, and the name which was later applied to the whole group – the 'pundits' – came from the first, Naim Singh, whose code name was 'pundit'. In 1864,

above

Like all the pundits, Kishen Singh was trained to take accurate measurements and observations with the minimum of equipment and fuss. They were given rosaries to keep track of the number of paces they took. No matter the terrain, each pace measured 84 cm (33 inches). The rosaries had 100 beads instead of the traditional 108. After every 100 paces, one bead would be clicked, and therefore a complete circuit of the rosary represented 10,000 paces, or 8.4 km (5.2 miles). The Tibetan prayer wheel, which normally consisted of strips of paper inscribed with holy prayers were modified so the surveyors could record their observations on them.

Naim Singh travelled as a horse dealer through Nepal to the Tibetan border aiming for Lhasa. After this attempt failed, he tried again as a spice dealer, and eventually reached Lhasa, where he undertook most of his work at night, for fear of being recognised. There he met both the Dalai and Panchen Lama, who were both children at the time, and went on to visit the sacred Lake Manasarowar. He calculated the height of Lhasa by boiling water. His estimation was 3,240 m (10,630 ft), just 200 m (655 ft) short! In this one journey, he covered 1,900 km (1,200 miles), returning to the Survey's station after 21 months away. Singh went on to investigate the Thok Jalung gold mines of western Tibet and the source of the Indus. He was presented with the Patron's Medal of the Royal Geographical Society, the highest medal the Society bestowed on a geographer.

Naim Singh was succeeded by other, equally successful 'pundits', notably Kishen Singh, his nephew, and Kintup. Kishen's fourth, and most successful, journey took him across the Tibetan Plateau to the Gobi desert with the objective of surveying the route north. Forced to travel in part by horse, Kishen Singh measured each of the animal's paces for 370 km (230 miles). On his way home, he visited most of the towns in the hitherto unknown eastern sector of Tibet, greatly increasing knowledge of the country. He had long been given up for dead, but returned to India after four years, having covered around 4,800 km (3,000 miles) and, amazingly, calculating his own position to within 15 km (9 miles).

Kintup, codenamed K.P., set out in 1880 as part of the search for the source of the Brahmaputra. The Tibetans claimed it was connected to the Tsangpo, and Kishen's task was to track the Tsangpo as far as he could and throw in some tagged logs. If the logs reached the observers on the Brahmaputra on the other side of the Himalayas, they would have discovered the two rivers were connected. To reduce his chance of detection, he attached himself as a servant to a Mongolian lama, who unfortunately decided to sell him to a Tibetan lama who kept a watchful eye on him. Asking to visit a distant shrine, K.P. made for the Tsangpo, where he hid 50 logs in a cave. Some months later, requesting permission for a further pilgrimage and having sent a message to the Survey that he was releasing the logs, he returned to throw them in. As a result of his frequent pilgrimages — what seemed his religious devotion — he was granted freedom from his masters. Upon his return to India four years after his departure, however, he learned that his message had never been delivered and all was in vain — the logs went completely unnoticed.

Of course, while the British were infiltrating Tibet from the south, the Russians enacted their part of the 'Great Game' from the north, through the equally inaccessible northern plateau. Nikolai Przhevalsky, a soldier, naturalist

The pundit Kintup was tasked with discovering whether the Tsangpo, photographed here, was connected with the mighty Brahmaputra. In fact, they are one and the same river, originating from a glacier in the northern Himalayas near the holy lake of Manasarowar and tumbling 3,000 km (4,800 miles) into the Bay of Bengal. It is the longest river in Tibet and the highest river on earth, with an average altitude of more than 4,000 m (13,100 ft). The photographer was Captain C. G. Rawling who took two expeditions into Tibet, the first into Central Tibet in 1903, and the second in 1904, when, as a detachment from Younghusband's Tibet mission, he explored and surveyed from Lhasa to Simla .

below right

The Tien Shan mountains are the product of the clash between the Eurasian and Indo-Australian plates, lying between China, Tadjikistan, Uzbekistan, Kazakhstan and Kyrgyzstan. To the semi-nomadic people who live in the mountains, they are called the Tengri Tag, or 'Mountains of the Spirits'. The range experiences frequent rainfall due to the proximity of the Taklamakan Desert.

above

The Przhevalsky horse, Mongolia's national symbol, is the only surviving species of wild horse, which once inhabited the vast grasslands of Central Asia. The species was first recorded by Colonel Nikolai Przhevalsky in 1881 near the edge of the Gobi desert, and subsequently given his name. News of his discovery spread throughout Russia, Europe and America, and as a result, over 50 foals were caught and transported to be kept by private individuals and zoos. All of the captive Przhevalsky's horses alive today are descended from just 13 of these captured horses. As a result of hunting, competition for decreasing land resources and interbreeding with Mongol ponies, numbers of the horse have decreased and, since the late 1960s, no Przhevalsky's have been seen in the wild. In 1977 the Foundation for the Preservation and Protection of the Przhevalsky Horse was founded to re-establish the species.

and keen hunter, was the only Russian who succeeded in getting close to its sacred capital. Though not making any substantial discoveries, he did add a huge amount of information to what was known of Central Asia at that time, being the first modern traveller to delineate the Astin Tagh mountains and also the first to survey the sources of the Hwang Ho River.

His first journey (1870–73) took him across Mongolia, through part of the Gobi Desert and via the Great Wall to Peking. From here, he assembled a small caravan to take him across the Ordos desert, following the Yellow river towards Lake Koko Nor, south of the Nan Shan mountains. At 3,200 m (10,500 ft) above sea level and halfway towards his goal, the encroaching winter and the sad state of his camel train forced Przhevalsky to turn back. After recuperation, he finally achieved his 'dream' and reached the lake in October 1872.

Przhevalsky was never to achieve his other aim, that of reaching Lhasa, despite two attempts. The second was thwarted by a Chinese rumour being spread in Lhasa that a Russian was planning to kidnap the Dalai Lama. Enraged, the Tibetans prevented him reaching the capital, just 250 km (170 miles) outside, and he was forced to retrace his steps; in doing so he embarked on a remarkable journey across the entire Gobi desert to the Russian border. While preparing for yet another expedition, Przhevalsky died in the Tien Shan mountains in 1888.

A combination of Przhevalsky's forays into Tibet and the news that a Russian agent had established a powerful influence in Lhasa reignited and magnified British interest in this area. This Russian agent – of Mongolian origin – had been a Buddhist monk, and therefore had access to the Potala Palace, eventually becoming tutor to the Dalai Lama himself. His influence was so great that, by 1902, the Dalai Lama was talking of visiting St Petersburg, and plans to link the two countries by a branch of the Trans-Siberian railway were being discussed. The British became increasingly nervous, and in 1903 Francis Younghusband, already an established explorer and soldier, was appointed to lead a mission to Lhasa.

above
Younghusband was a classic player in 'The Great Game', a term immortalised in Rudyard Kipling's book *Kim*, to describe over 100 years of intrigue, military adventurism and espionage. At the onset of the 'Game' between Britain and Russia, the two countries were separated by 3,200 km (2,000 miles); by the end, Russian outposts were within 32 km (20 miles) of India. Younghusband is pictured second from the left in the front row.

Born in India, Younghusband's credentials as a traveller were second to none. In the 1880s, he had travelled from Peking to India with the purpose of pioneering a new trade route between Peking and Kashgar. His journey took him across the Gobi desert and Kashgar and he became the first European to cross the Muztag Pass in the Karakorams and over the next 10 years, he continued to travel throughout India. Like most travellers at that time, he was fascinated with Lhasa – the forbidden city – and its mystical peoples.

above

The Tibet Mission Force, led by Younghusband in 1904, heralded a series of invasions and power struggles over Tibet. In 1911, the Republic of China was established which declared Tibet to be a province of China. In 1949 the newly formed People's Republic of China invaded and in 1953 the Tibetan spiritual leader, the Dalai Lama, escaped into exile.

Though it was called a 'diplomatic' mission, Younghusband travelled with thousands of soldiers. Greeted in southern Tibet with the message that the Tibetans would never negotiate with Britain, Younghusband marched on until reaching the Guru Plain, where they were met by a considerable Tibetan force. Although neither side seemed willing to open fire, one chance shot led to firing from both sides and as they were no military match for the British, the Tibetans suffered heavily. Upon reaching Lhasa – the first Europeans to do since Huc and Gabet – they found the Dalai Lama had fled, and his Regent had no choice but to give in to Younghusband's demands. The British soon realised, however, that maintaining a garrison in Lhasa would be almost impossible, and so they modified the treaty that Younghusband's had signed with the Regent. To solve Britain's problem and prevent Russia from moving back in, China was given sovereignty over Tibet. Thus, the 'Great Game' which had been played out over Tibet was over.

Exploration of this region, of course, had not been exhausted. Two other important figures in this period and region were Sven Hedin and Aurel Stein. Born in Sweden, Hedin was inspired by the books and stories of James Fenimore Cooper, Livingstone and Nordenskiöld, and was certain of his destiny from a young age. In 1890, as a member of the Swedish embassy in Persia, he travelled to Kashgar across

right

'The whole Asia was open before me. I felt that I had been called to make discoveries without limits – they just waited for me in the middle of the deserts and mountain peaks. During those three years, that my journey took, my first guiding principle was to explore only such regions, where nobody else has been earlier.' Sven Hedin writing of his 1893 journey. Hedin's reputation was later to be questioned and disparaged by his countrymen following his support and admiration of the Nazis and Hitler, whom he met and with whom he had long conversations about politics. He was also approving of Mao, of whom he said, 'Mao is the best thing that has happened to China in a thousand years.' The Swedish Nobel prize-winner Harry Martinson called Hedin an 'imperialist who happened to be born in a small country'.

the Tien Shan mountains. This whetted his appetite for adventure and between 1893 and 1894, Hedin travelled to Tashkent via the Pamirs in midwinter, accompanied by Khirzig tribesmen. His inexperience, however, was to take him almost too close to the edge. In the midst of the Taklamakan Desert, he realised his caravan was running out of water, and considered turning back. But, urged on by his guides, who believed the river they were aiming for, the Khotan, was near, they continued into one of the most inhospitable deserts on earth.

With a strictly rationed water supply, Hedin pressed on, but as days became a week, and their water supplies ran out and with still no sign of the river, two of his men and all of the animals died. In desperation, the men tried to drink the blood of their sheep, but this also proved impossible, as it

above

Sven Hedin's photo *c.* 1907 shows the brother- and sister-in-law of the Tashi Lama, also known as the Panchen Lama. During this time, Hedin became friends with the Tashi Lama, who had become the most important man in Tibet after the Dalai Lama had been forced to flee following Younghusband's mission in 1904.

above right

Marc Aurel Stein, the Hungarian-born English archaeologist, was responsible for unearthing the cities of the Silk Road from the sand. He wrote reports and letters once a week even from the middle of the Taklamakan Desert where in the winter it was so cold that his ink froze in its pot. The famous archaeologist Leonard Woolley said of Stein that he conducted 'the most daring and adventuresome raid upon the ancient world that any archaeologist has attempted'. As well as his uncovering of the Silk Road cities, Stein also conducted the first archaeological surveys of Iran and Iraq and pioneered the use of aerial photography in archaeology.

coagulated so quickly. Gradually, all the men died, save Hedin and one servant, Kasim. Dragging themselves across the desert, they at last sighted the line of trees which signalled the river's presence, but Kasim could not make it. Hedin reached the river only to find that it was dry, but at his last gasp, heard a splash and saw a bird fly up from a pool. He filled his boots with water to take back to Kasim, whom he managed to revive, and they were later rescued by shepherds.

This incident did not deter him, and Hedin was to cross the Taklamakan Desert again almost immediately after returning to Kashgar. It was during this crossing that he discovered decayed timber posts in the sand, which upon further investigation turned out to be an ancient Silk Road city; and he was to discover two more *en route* to the Gobi Desert.

Between 1900 and 1901, during the time it was closed to Europeans, Hedin made two failed attempts to reach Lhasa, but it is for his fourth expedition in 1906 that he is perhaps most well-known. From Leh, he crossed the Himalayas in winter *en route* to explore the Tsangpo River Valley, which flows through southern Tibet. Following the river to the east, he visited the monastery of Tasilhumpo, which was home to some 3,000 lamas. From here, Hedin was to make two highly significant discoveries: firstly, the source of the Tsangpo in a glacier high up in the Tibetan mountains, and secondly, the source of the Indus River just north of Lake Manasarowar in the south-west of Tibet. It is for these discoveries that Hedin is regarded as one of Tibet's most important explorers.

below
'I ascended the highest dune near our camp and, carefully
scanning the horizon, saw nothing but the same expanse
of formidable sand-ridges, like huge waves of an angry
ocean suddenly arrested in movement. There was a
strange allurement in this vista, suggesting Nature in the
contortions of death.' Stein, as reported in Sven Hedin's
My Life as an Explorer. The photo shows Stein's camels
in the Taklamakan Desert during his second Central Asian
expedition, 1907.

below top

Pictured is a part of the interior of a ruined fort in the Lop Desert. The area was excavated by Stein during his third expedition in February 1914. Stein came to this area as a result of Sven Hedin's maps and uncovered Loulan, an ancient garrison town, which protected China's western frontier and the Silk Road traffic. There, Stein discovered many coins, documents and pottery. The Lop Desert has since been used by China to test its nuclear weapons.

below bottom

After Stein's first expedition, the wealth of the ancient Silk Road became an international search. In 1902, just two months after Stein's first expedition, Germany and Japan sought to unearth their share of Chinese treasures. The quest was to involve archaeologists from seven countries and lasted over a quarter of a century. The artefacts removed are now found throughout 30 museums across Europe, America, Russia and East Asia. The photo shows Stein with his assistants at Kara-Khoka during his third expedition in 1915.

Having been inspired by Hedin's account of ancient cities in the Taklamakan Desert, a Hungarian contemporary named Marc Aurel Stein travelled to Asia to explore further its mysteries. After preliminary investigations in 1900, Stein returned to the Desert in 1906 with a large expeditionary team. Their work uncovered complex frontier towns, proving that thousands of years previously, what was now desert had been fertile plain, traversed by rivers and trade routes. The relics they found showed evidence of both Buddhist, Chinese, and Greek and Roman influence, suggesting the trade routes had reached from China to Greece and Rome. The same intense dry heat which made Stein's work difficult and dangerous had preserved these ancient cities and their secrets until this important discovery at the beginning of the 20th century.

As he moved across to the western edge of the desert, Stein was also to find an early portion of the Great Wall. But it was near here, just outside the Chinese frontier town of Dunhuang, that Stein was to make perhaps his most spectacular find. On a towering cliff, great temples had been carved into the rock face, behind which were networks of caves that were beginning to crumble away. Stein persuaded the monk who looked after the caves to sell him some recently discovered ancient manuscripts, and rolls of fine Chinese silk paintings, sacred texts and temple banners which were removed under the cover of darkness and later donated to the British Museum. Although many Chinese and western scholars have not forgiven the removal of these items from China, others argue that the subsequent disappearance of many others which remained was sufficient vindication.

In all, Stein travelled throughout the Hindu Kush and Gobi Desert areas for 30 years. Stein's and Hedin's paths were to meet several times in Central Asia over this period as they both continued their exploration. They were the last significant explorers to travel this region before the Communist Party tightened its grip on even the remote reaches of its empire and signalled the end of an era of adventure and discovery.

ARABIA

The political games played between Russian and Britain over Central Asia were also played out in the southerly deserts of Arabia. But exploration in this region was not just politically motivated. This was the Orient, and many came here to explore its fascinating and exotice cultures, and the geographically extreme landscape that dominated it.

From the 1700s until 1818, the Heart of Arabia – the Nejd – had been difficult to travel in, partly as a result of the Wahhabi sect. This extreme form of Islam was founded in 1703 by Abd al-Wahhab and its aversion to Europeans meant this area was particularly hostile to them. Coupled with the extreme geography to the north, east and south which consists of stretches of hostile desert, and to the west the holy cities forbidden to non-believers, the Nejd virtually unknown to Europe. However, in 1818, the Egyptian army defeated the Wahhabis and around the mid-1800s, a small number of explorers began to infiltrate the country.

One of the first of these explorers was William Palgrave, a British traveller, scholar and author, as well as being a Jesuit priest and spy for the French. Born in England, Palgrave was educated at Trinity College, Oxford, where he distinguished himself in Literature. Immediately after university, he served in India, but soon found this unfulfilling and was ordained as a Jesuit priest, working as a missionary in Southern India. From India, he turned his attentions to Syria where he became an expert not only in Arabic culture and custom, but also in Islam and the Koran. It was for this knowledge that Palgrave was hired by the French emperor to gain intelligence of a little-known yet fascinating world.

In 1862, Palgrave, travelling as a Syrian doctor and accompanied by a Syrian companion, crossed the An Nafud, the desert which protects the Nejd from the north. In his writings, he describes experiencing the desert storm, forcing their party and camels down to the floor as the hot, powerful wind swept burning sand across them:

'So dark was the atmosphere and so burning the heat, that it seemed that hell had risen from the earth, or descended from above. But we were yet in time, and at the moment when the worst of the concentrated poison-blast was coming around, we were already prostrate one and all within the tent, almost suffocated indeed, but safe; while our camels lay without like the dead, their long necks stretched out on the sand awaiting the passing of the gale.'

above

William Gifford Palgrave travelled in Arabia gathering intelligence for France. In his introduction to his *Personal Narrative of a Year's Journey* published in 1868, he wrote of his object of interest in Arabia: 'the men of the land, rather than the land of the men, were my main object of research and principal study. My attention was directed to the moral, intellectual, and political conditions of living Arabia, rather than to the physical phenomena of the country – of great indeed, but, to me, of inferior interest.'

From the Nejd they travelled to Riyadh, at that time the centre of the remaining Wahhabi sect, where he narrowly escaped death, and onto Al Qatif on the Gulf. The flamboyant literary style of his account of his journey and his remark that he had left 'much untold' – presumably intelligence for the French – led many to be highly suspicious of his tales.

One of the next, and certainly most well-respected explorers to travel this region was Charles Montague Doughty. He was, and is, regarded by many – including T. E. Lawrence – to be one of the most important Arabian explorers of all time. In the 1870s he spent two years in Arabia, firstly with the *Hajj* pilgrimage and then with the Bedouin, the nomadic tribes of the desert. He was unusual in that he refused to conceal his identity and his beliefs as a Christian, something previous explorers, notably Burton and Palgrave, had successfully attempted. Despite wearing his differences on his sleeve, Doughty was to share the life of the tribesmen he lived with almost completely. He slept, ate and argued with them and experienced both their friendship and generosity as well as the extremity and cruelty of their desert. In *Travels in Arabia Deserta*, Doughty described the fate of those who fell ill during a passage across the desert:

'The lonely and indigent man, and without succour, who falls in the empty wilderness, he is desolate indeed. When the great convoy is passed from him, and he is forsaken of all mankind, if any Beduw find him fainting, it is but likely they will strip him, seeing he is not yet dead. The dead corpses unburied are devoured by hyenas which follow the ill odour of the caravan. There is little mercy in those Ageyl [soldiers] who ride after; none upon the road will do a gentle deed but for silver.'

Doughty considered himself first and foremost a poet, and following his travels he settled down to his 'true work', publishing various works of poetry and fiction, but all the time his work was inspired by his experiences in the desert. He was a traditional writer, and his Victorian style had its many critics, yet he was determined to rescue the English language from what he saw as its decadent, modern influences. This same attitude led him to mourn the passing of traditional desert culture and customs. Like Thesiger some decades after him, he was upset by the 'civilised' world encroaching upon the harsh but admirable ways of the Bedouin.

Doughty's account of his time in the desert, *Travels in Arabia Deserta*, was to become a bible for those who had a fascination for the desert and is considered a seminal work to this day. At the time, his style was little appreciated but for a few, and it is T. E. Lawrence who is credited for bringing it to the attention of a wider audience and restoring his reputation. In his introduction to an edition published in 1932, Lawrence admitted he found it 'not comfortable' to write about the book, it being 'something particular, a bible of its kind'. He went on to say 'I do not think that any traveller in Arabia before or after Mr Doughty has qualified himself to praise the book, much less to blame it.' His legacy was lasting and on his tombstone, as seems apt, is written 'poet, patriot and explorer'.

Gertrude Margaret Lowthian Bell, 'The Uncrowned Queen of Iraq', was once one of the most influential women in the British Empire, particularly with regard to Arabia. Born in the English countryside in 1868, she became interested in the Middle East on a visit to an uncle who was an ambassador in Persia, and this first journey became the basis for a book, *Persian Pictures*. After mountaineering in the Alps and travelling in Europe and Turkey, she longed to return to the Middle East. Here, she was to journey in various parts of Arabia and Persia, excavating and mapping the ruins of Byzantine and Christian churches.

As a result of this mapping and knowledge of previously uncharted areas, she became invaluable in

above
'They tell tales of him, making something of the tall and impressive figure, very wise and gentle, who came to them like a herald of the outside world … They say that he seemed proud of only being a Christian, and yet never crossed their faith. He was book-learned, but simple in the arts of living, ignorant of camels, trustful of every man, very silent …'
T. E. Lawrence's *Introduction* to *Travels in Arabia Deserta*

World War I and was the only woman to be employed in the Intelligence Service there. This relationship continued after the war and Bell was instrumental in the creation of the new Iraqi nation and its political identity. For many years, she was a close adviser to its first ruler, King Faisal. She developed such an understanding and knowledge of the desert that she was awarded the Royal Geographical Society's Gold Medal for Exploration. Her personal life, however, was not so smooth, and Bell committed suicide in Baghdad in 1926.

This area was further opened up to the western mind by the journeys and

below

Bell hated any form of publicity or 'advertisement' as she called it and wrote home: 'Please, please don't supply information about me or photographs of me to newspaper correspondents … I hate the whole advertisement business. I always throw all letters (fortunately they're not many in number) asking for an interview or a photograph straight in the wastepaper basket.'

below

'Few moments of exhilaration can come as that which stands at the threshold of wild travel,' Gertrude Bell wrote. The knowledge and associations she had developed whilst travelling throughout Persia, Iraq and Syria lead her to become one of the most powerful women in the British Empire. She was later to be integral to the creation of Iraq, where she became one of King Faisal's closest advisers. 'I don't care to be in London much. I like Baghdad, and I like Iraq. It's the real East and it's stirring; things are happening here, and the romance of it all touches me and absorbs me.' This photo shows Bell's tent at camp in Urzeh, Iraq.

right

'It is, I believe, a fallacy to think of travellers' qualities as physical. If I had to write a decalogue for journeys, eight out of ten virtues should be moral, and I should put first of all a temper as serene at the end as at the beginning of the day. Then would come the capacity to accept values and to judge by standards other than our own. The rapid judgment of character; and a love of nature, which must include human nature also. The power to disassociate oneself from one's own bodily sensations. A knowledge of the local history and language. A leisurely and uncensorious mind. A tolerable constitution and the capacity to eat and sleep at any moment. And lastly, and especially here, a quickness in repartee.'
The Southern Gates of Arabia, Freya Stark.

writings of Freya Madeline Stark. Attracted to the 'blank spots' on maps of the Middle East, Stark was drawn to the 'lure of exploration' as she called it, and was to retain this wandering spirit until her late eighties, searching both for archaeological ruins and a sense of change and contrast:

'If I were asked the most agreeable thing in life, I should say it is the pleasure of contrast. One cannot imagine anyone but an angel sitting with a harp in Paradise forever. The ordinary human being needs a change. This is the secret charm of the oasis, usually an indifferent patch of greenery made precious solely by surrounding sands.'

She moved to San Remo, Italy in 1921, where she learnt Arabic from a monk, on her premise that the

'most interesting things in the world were likely to happen in the neighbourhood of oil'. Upon her first
sight of the desert and its camels, she was at once struck: 'I never imagined that my first sight of the
desert would come as such a shock of beauty and enslave me right away.' This was in Lebanon, and in
The Freya Stark Story she describes her rapid realisations that 'the whole of my future must be
rearranged'.

Stark made the Middle East her home. In preparation for her next voyage and with her Arabic now
fluent, she began to learn Persian, and in 1930 travelled to the famous 'Valley of the Assassins'. Her
time in the valley, searching for archaeological ruins, was described in her book, *The Valley of the
Assassins*, and on her return to London she was presented with both the Royal Geographical Society's
Back Medal and the Burton Medal of the Royal Asiatic Society.

In the following years, lured by various reports of ancient ruins and long-lost towns and cities of the
silk and incense trade, Stark travelled throughout Persia and to the Hadramaut, the southern province
of Yemen. The Hadramaut in particular, which she explored in search of the ancient frankincense route,
was an area riven by tribal warfare and largely unexplored.

As a result of her linguistic and cultural knowledge of Arabia and Persia, Stark was employed in
British Intelligence in World War II. Over the next few decades, she wrote three books of her travels and
continued travelling – to Turkey, Afghanistan and Nepal. As a writer, geographer, archaeologist and
historian and, above all, as a woman, she was, and remains, a source of inspiration.

THE EMPTY QUARTER

The Empty Quarter, the Rub' al Khali, or the Abode of Emptiness, was not fully explored by westerners until the early part of the 20th century. At 400,000 square kilometres (250,000 square miles), it is the largest contiguous sand desert in the world, where temperatures routinely measure in the late 50 degrees centigrade (over 135 fahrenheit), where humidity can be as low as two per cent and sand dunes can reach up 330 metres (1,100 ft) high. The outskirts of the desert are home to the Bedouin, the tribespeople who accompanied many of the explorers of this region on their journeys. Their way of life was, and still is, a hard and physical one, as T. E. Lawrence alluded to in his *The Seven Pillars of Wisdom*:

> 'Bedouin ways were hard, even for those brought up in them, and for strangers, terrible: a death in life.'

Not only is the desert physically extreme, but as in much Arabian exploration of this period, the presence of hostile tribes combined to make the crossing of the Empty Quarter massively challenging; as Thesiger said, 'the fine and greatest prize of Arabian exploration'. The challenge was considered so great that only two years before it was successfully completed, T. E. Lawrence was to remark, 'only an airship could cross it'.

This last region of Arabia to be explored by Europeans turned into a race between two Englishmen: Bertram Thomas and Harry St John Philby. Both were in the service of the British government at the time, Thomas as minister for the Sultan of Muscat, and Philby, who converted to Islam, as an adviser to King Saud of Saudi Arabia.

above

The Rub' al Khali, or Empty Quarter, occupies much of the south-central part of the Arabian peninsula. It is now virtually waterless, and rain can sometimes not fall for years. Archaeological and geological studies have shown that as recently as 40,000 years ago, it was an area of lakes and rivers, where animals like hippopotamus and water buffalo thrived. Today, wildlife is confined to species that are specially adapted to conditions of extreme aridity. Until recently, only Bedu tribes such as the Awamir, Manahil and Rashid travelled in and across 'The Sands', as they called them.

Thomas set out from Dhofar on the Arabian Sea heading north with a Bedouin escort in December 1930. Their route took them over the Hadramaut mountains behind Dhofar and out to where the shifting sand dunes of the Empty Quarter proper begin. Faced with possible attack from raiders, and severe sandstorms, Thomas and his party crossed the 430 km (270 miles) from Shanna to the northern fringe of the Empty Quarter in 18 days, travelling at an average of 24 km (15 miles) per day.

above

The photo shows the procession of Harry St John Philby's party across the sand during his crossing of the Empty Quarter. Philby has latterly become better known because of his son, Kim Philby, who was a double agent for the Soviet Union. He defected in 1963, his case generating a huge amount of publicity.

Philby, who had considered it his task to be the first European to cross the Empty Quarter, was extremely disappointed when he heard he had been beaten by Thomas. In fact, circumstances had prevented him leaving that same winter, when the Saudi government had refused him time to make his crossing. He nevertheless set out in January 1932, and made a more spectacular attempt.

Crossing from north to south, beginning in Al Hufuf, Philby's party made the mistake of overloading their camels. Zigzagging south, they were 160 km (100 miles) from Shanna when their entire party, including the camels, began to suffer from heat and exhaustion. Backtracking to Naifa, they were to rest there before Philby made another attempt with a smaller party westward some weeks later. They reached As Sulayyil after travelling on average 65 km (40 miles) per day, a journey which prompted Philby to call crossing the Empty Quarter 'an adventure not to be lightly undertaken by the faint-hearted'.

The last in the line of 'traditional' explorers of Arabia was Wilfred Thesiger. The son of a British minister, he was born in Addis Ababa, Ethiopia in 1910. He left for England as a young man to study at Eton and Oxford, but in the 1930s he returned to work in the Civil Service in the Sudan and then served in the Middle East in World War II, part of this in the SAS. Following the war, he gathered information as part of a locust-control project, and it was through the forays into the desert in his work that he became fascinated by the Bedu and their homeland.

opposite

His superior in the Civil Service in Sudan called Wilfred Thesiger a 'brave, awkward, attractive creature'. In *Arabian Sands* Thesiger said: 'No man can live this life and emerge unchanged. He will carry, however faint, the imprint of the desert, the brand which marks the nomad; and he will have within him the yearning to return, weak or inconsistent according to his nature. For this cruel land can cast a spell which no temperate clime can match.'

Thesiger crossed the Empty Quarter twice, with members of the Bait Khatir and Rashid tribes, the latter being the same tribe that had accompanied Bertram Thomas on his crossing. From the beginning, irritated that they should treat him any differently from their own, Thesiger rejected offers to ride as they walked, or to drink whilst they abstained. His journeys were made in secret, without permission, and so his party avoided desert tribes and, if challenged, attempted to pass Thesiger off as an Arab. He had the added worry of remaining out of the gaze of a group of extreme anti-Christians in northern Oman, who hearing of a previous journey through their territory, were determined he should never pass through again.

below

'For me, exploration was a personal venture. I did not go to the Arabian desert to collect plants nor to make a map; such things were incidental … I went there to find peace in the company of desert peoples. I set myself a goal on these journeys, and although the goal itself was unimportant, its attainment had to be worth every effort and sacrifice … I would not myself have wished to cross the Empty Quarter in a car. Luckily this was impossible when I did my journeys, for to have done the journey on a camel when I could have done it in a car would have turned the venture into a stunt.'

His second journey was, of course, more ambitious than his first, both in terms of the route and the smaller party he took to evade detection – six men as opposed to 13. It was on this second trip that he noticed the desert landscape was already changing: in the distance he saw a car carrying none other than St John Philby on his way to meet Thesiger. Resisting King Ibn Saud's refusal to allow them across some of his route, Thesiger's luck ran out when he was arrested, but an interception from Philby was to set him and his companions free. After his two journeys across the Empty Quarter, increasing resistance to his movements were to cause him to leave a place he had learnt to understand and love; as he says in *Arabian Sands*: 'I know how it felt to go into exile.'

His instinctive sense of a hostile world is what he says drove him to his journeys in the desert and the friendships he developed with the Bedu. In *Arabian Sands*, he described this search for comradeship:

'The Empty Quarter offered me the chance to win distinction as a traveller; but I believed that it could give me more than this, that in those empty wastes I could find the comradeship that comes with solitude, and, among the Bedu, comradeship in a hostile world. … Many who venture into dangerous places have found this comradeship among members of their own race; a few find it more easily among people from other lands, the very differences which separate them binding them ever more closely. I found it among the Bedu. Without it, these journeys would have been a meaningless penance.'

Like Doughty, from whose *Travels in Arabia Deserta* he drew inspiration, Thesiger was painfully aware of the changes that were sweeping these desert peoples and worried about the loss of culture and custom that ultimately would mean. He had a deep and respectful understanding of the Bedu with whom he spent many years. He says of their character in his classic, *Arabian Sands*, 'how often I was humbled by those illiterate herdsmen who possessed, in so much greater measure than I, generosity and courage, endurance, patience and light-hearted gallantry. Among no other people have I felt the same sense of personal inferiority'.

In 1951, Thesiger went to the marshes of Iraq with the intention of staying two weeks to shoot duck. He was to stay seven years, spending the summers with the Kurds in the north; his resulting book, *The Marsh Arabs*, like its predecessor, was hailed a classic. Where in the Empty Quarter he had been an explorer, he now became more of a doctor and adviser to the Marsh Arabs, but despite his work, the increasingly difficult political situation forced him again to leave. He was later to travel in Pakistan, Afghanistan and Africa.

Thesiger's years in the desert marked the end of an era. Between his journeys, he estimates that he covered over 65,000 km (40,000 miles), almost twice the distance around the globe. His books, considered classics in the league of *Travels in Arabia Deserta*, are a fitting testament to the native people of this land and their life, which has since changed irrevocably. Thesiger, who attempted, possibly more than any other explorer of this region, to live and travel as the Bedu lived and travelled, was also the last.

NORTH AFRICA

The tales of the mythical oasis of Zarzura date as
far back as the *1001 Arabian Nights*. Supposedly
located deep within the Sahara, its springs were
believed to flow year-round and as with all
mythical places, it was thought to possess the
untold wealth of an ancient civilisation.

In January 1923 Ahmed Hassanein Bey, an
aristocratic Egyptian explorer backed by the Royal
Geographical Society, set out to find the oasis
somewhere in the uncharted hinterland of the
desert on the modern-day Egypt–Libya border.
Starting from the Egyptian port of Sollum on the
Mediterranean coast with a camel caravan,
Hassanein Bey crossed the Libyan Plateau and
descended into the Great Sand Sea that separates
the Qatar Depression from the Kufra Oasis. This
part of the journey was familiar to him, as
Hassanein had visited Kufra at the end of 1920,
accompanied by the intrepid English woman
explorer, Rosita Forbes, who had travelled
disguised as a Bedouin woman.

From Kufra, the expedition travelled south-
east and further into the Libyan Desert. They
journeyed by night, setting off at about 9.30pm,
stopping at seven in the morning. On a good
night, they could cover up to 65 km (40 miles).
Four months after having left the coast, the
caravan could make out a mountain some 450 m
(1,500 ft) high. Here they came across the 'lost
oasis' of Arkenu.

Further to the south-east, however, came
the climax of the expedition. At Uweinat,
another 'lost oasis' was found, but in caves in
the side of the large massif, Hassanein came
across a series of spectacular cave paintings.
Lions, giraffes, ostriches, all kinds of gazelle
and some cow-like creatures were represented,
but no camels.

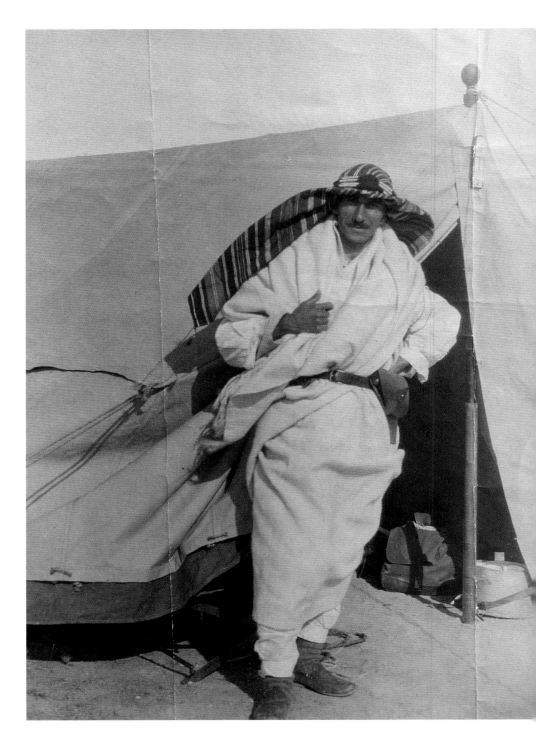

below
Engravings in the valley
of Karkur Talh. One of
the finds was the 'Cave
of Swimmers', later
made famous in the film
The English Patient. The
drawings showed that at
some time – now

believed to be some
6,000 years ago – there
had been water in the
Sahara.

right
The well at Uweinat.
Here the expedition
found safe, fresh water.

At the previous oasis,
Arkenu, the water was
contaminated and had
given three of the men
dysentery. They had had
to be carried on the
backs of camels, which
were already exhausted
and overloaded.

After exploring the wells and caves of Uweinat, the expedition pressed on, eventually reaching El Fasher in the Sudan, nearly 1,600 km (1,000 miles) from the coast. As the caravan finally left the desert behind, Hassanein Bey experienced misgivings familiar to travellers who have survived a journey though one of the great deserts: 'I realised with a stab of regret that this was my last day in the real desert,' he wrote later. 'I thought how I should miss my men and my camels, the desolateness and the beauty, the solitude and the companionship – in two words, the desert and its life. I thanked God for his guidance across this vast expanse of pathless sand, and found myself adding a prayer, half wistfully, that I might come back to it again.'

Hassanein Bey's account of the journey was published in London in the *Geographical Journal*, the *National Geographic Magazine*, and in a book, *The Lost Oases*.

below

below

The image shows Mount Sonder looking north-east.
Mount Sonder is in the Western Macdonnell Ranges near
Alice Springs. It was first sighted by Ernest Giles in 1872,
as he explored central Australia west from the Overland
Telegraph line. In 1873 he embarked on a second trip
westwards, and in 1875 he crossed from South Australia
to Western Australia through the Great Victoria Desert.
The photo was taken by C. T. Madigan (1927–30).

AUSTRALIA

Exploration of Australia's vast, arid and inhospitable interior was a 19th-century phenomenon. While
Australia's coast was discovered during the 17th and 18th centuries and the first European settlement
was established in New South Wales in 1788, the interior of the continent remained largely uncharted.
It was not until the 19th century that explorers ventured into this extreme landscape and traversed the
continent, motivated most certainly by notions of heroism and glory but also, as Captain Charles Sturt
wrote, 'A wish to contribute to the public good.' Exploration of this landscape was vital: it created the
possibility of cross-country communication, it opened up transport and trade routes and it found new,
fertile and rich land for British colonisation.

In 1828, Australia was afflicted by a terrible drought, prompting a severe crop failure of such a serious
nature that Sturt was sent by Governor Darling on an expedition into the previously unexplored central

territory in the hope of finding well-watered land. Sturt traced the path of the Macquarie River, proceeding past the marshes that a previous explorer, Oxley, had deemed to be the termination of the river. Sturt proved this to be false when he discovered that the Macquarie joined a new river, which he loyally named the Darling, after his Governor. On his second expedition he discovered that both the Murrumbidgee and the Darling flowed into a much larger and grander river that Sturt named the Murray, after Sir George Murray, Secretary of State for War and the Colonies. Floating down the Murray in a whaleboat, Sturt and his men were swept finally into Lake Alexandria, and to the west the explorers caught a glimpse of the sea at Encounter Bay. They had found the mouth of the river. His discovery was invaluable but he was unwilling to stop there.

His next goal was to reach the very centre of the continent and, aware of the risks this journey would entail, he wrote that it would be, 'a fearful but a splendid enterprise … if I fell my name would stand in a list I have always envied'. Sturt had observed the flight of migratory birds, noticing that they returned, healthy, every spring, and he came to the conclusion that there must be fertile lands in the interior. However, as opposed to the last one, this expedition was marked with disaster. Extreme drought trapped Sturt and his men in intolerable conditions for six months at Rocky Glen and one of Sturt's party, a man named Poole, died of scurvy. Only 240 km (150 miles) from the centre of Australia, Sturt was forced to turn back and abandon the expedition, defeated by the stony desert, the heat and his sense of responsibility for his men. 'On every play the curtain falls at last,' Sturt wrote in a letter, believing that his career as an explorer was at its end. Sadly, he was proved right.

However, while he had not reached the centre of Australia, he had discovered an important route, which led to the success of future explorers such as John McDouall Stuart. But perhaps the highlight of Sturt's career was the discovery of the Darling and the Murray. Sturt contributed vital information and mapped out this great waterway network that traversed Western Australia, therefore paving the way for further British colonisation into the interior.

John McDouall Stuart was an invaluable and respected member of Sturt's final expedition and became his second-in-command after Poole died of scurvy. On this expedition Stuart gained vital experience and developed his love of the interior territory, and it was this that inspired him to go back and complete Sturt's failed mission to reach the centre of Australia. In April 1860, Stuart succeeded in reaching the centre and camped at a red sandstone hill which he named 'Central Mount Sturt'. He chose this name 'after my excellent and esteemed commander of the expedition in 1844 and 1845, Captain Sturt'. However this name was changed to 'Central Mount Stuart' later and this is the name that appears on most Australian maps. In 1861, Stuart set out to traverse the continent south to north and while he succeeded, he took far longer than his contemporaries, Robert O'Hara Burke and William John Wills. However, unlike them, Stuart managed to survive the expedition.

above
Burke's expedition consisted of enough food to last for two years, six tonnes of firewood, 28 horses and wagons, 24 camels, 80 pairs of shoes, 20 camp beds, 30 cabbage tree hats, 57 buckets, brandy, preserved fruit, vegetables, firearms, and beads to give as gifts to the aborigines. Despite this, Burke's lack of leadership, inadequacies as a bushman and impatience were to result in both his and Wills's deaths. (National Library of Australia).

opposite

John Forrest (pictured here) and his brother Alexander were born in Bunbury, Western Australia. In 1890, John became the first Premier of Western Australia. He was later elected to the federal government in 1901 and was made Baron John Forrest of Bunbury in 1918. He also gave his name to the John Forrest National Park, 26 km (16 miles) east of Perth. (National Library of Australia).

It was Robert O'Hara Burke's and William John Wills's expedition that was perhaps one of the most famous, and ultimately tragic, expeditions into the interior territories. Their objective was to cross Australia, south to north from Melbourne to the Gulf of Carpentaria, and there was a great deal riding on their success. Aside from the prestige and glory in completing this journey there was a princely reward of 2,000 pounds and, as John McDouall Stuart had already departed on this mission, Burke was in a hurry.

Burke was born in Ireland in 1821 and migrated to Australia where he became an inspector of police in the gold mining areas. Despite courage and ambition he had little experience of such expeditions. Luckily Wills, a surveyor, was part of this expedition and brought a great deal more experience and knowledge with him. Progress was slow and so Robert O'Hara Burke became impatient and decided to ride ahead with eight men to Cooper's Creek (discovered by Sturt 30 years before). They waited six weeks for the rest of the party to catch up and when they failed to appear Burke decided to push on with three men, King, Gray and Wills, leaving Brahe and three others with strict orders to wait for their return.

The forward party trekked through blistering heat and tempestuous gales until they reached the Estuary of the Flinders River on the Gulf of Carpentaria on 9 February, exhausted and weakened by the harsh conditions and lack of food. On the return journey to Cooper's Creek, Burke accused Gray of stealing food and flogged him. Just a short time after this, Gray died of dysentery. On 21 April, the men arrived back at Cooper's Creek to find it deserted, Brahe and his men having departed just hours before. Brahe had left supplies but these soon ran out and the men became weaker and weaker, existing for weeks on nardoo seeds and fish given to them by Aborigines. Both Burke and Wills died of starvation and exposure on the banks of Cooper's Creek. Wills's last entry in his diary reads, 'My pulse are (sic) at forty eight, and very weak, and my legs and arms are nearly skin and bone. I can look out like Mr Micawber, "for something to turn up"'.

The next noteworthy Australian explorer was Colonel Peter Warburton. He served with the military in India until 1852 when he retired and emigrated to Adelaide with his family in 1853. He had a love of exploration and in 1872 he left Adelaide and travelled to Alice Springs, following the route established by Stuart in 1868. He left Alice Springs in 1873 and pushed on to the west coast where he arrived after extreme hardships with only three of his train of 18 camels still alive. Warburton nearly starved on this journey and spent part of the journey strapped at full length to his camel. In fact, it was the camel, with

above

Peter Egerton Warburton was born in 1813 at Northwich, England and educated in France. Before retiring to Australia in 1853, he served in the Navy in 1825 for four years, then transferred to the military at the Honourable East India Company's Military College. He served in India until 1852, beginning in the Bombay Army in 1831 as a subaltern and becoming Adjutant to the Marine Battalion, Bombay. He worked in the Adjutant General's Department and rose through its ranks until he attained his majority and became Deputy Adjutant General. Warburton returned to England in 1874, after an absence of over 40 years, but found the climate not to his taste and returned to Australia in a matter of weeks.

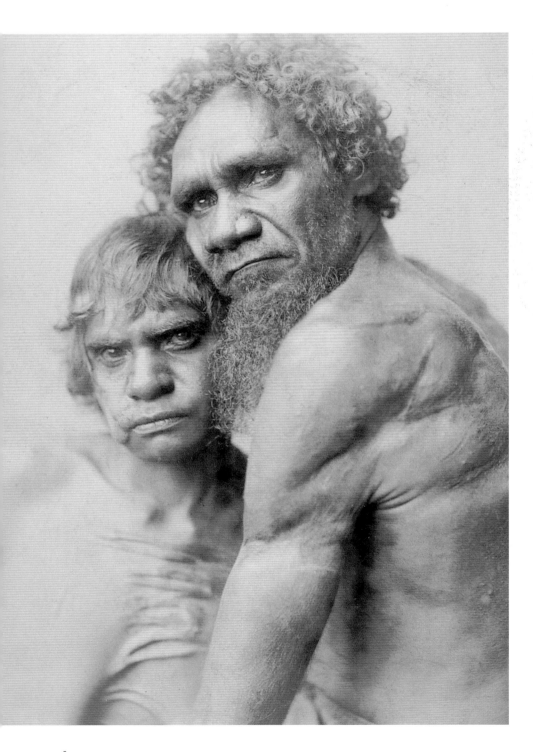

its innate ability to survive on little water and food that saved this expedition. During this journey, the true value of the camel to Australian exploration became acutely apparent.

At the age of 22, John Forrest and his brother Alexander made an expedition to explore the interior. Their aim was to find any traces or clues that would help them discover what had happened to the Prussian explorer Ludwig Leichhardt, who had vanished with six companions into the desert some years earlier on a mission to traverse Australia east to west. The Forrest brothers found little evidence of this previous expedition and the fate of Ludwig Leichhardt remains one of the unsolved mysteries of Australian land exploration. However, John Forrest and his brother spent 19 weeks in the interior and travelled over 3,200 km (2,000 miles) across previously uncharted territory discovering Lake Barlee and Mounts Ida, Leonara, Malcolm and Margaret. On arriving back in Perth, Forrest reported that he thought there were minerals in the area he had explored. He was to be proved right and today some of the richest mines in the world are found there.

But perhaps Forrest's crowning achievement was in 1874 when he crossed Australia from east to west on horseback. His predecessor, Warburton, had made this journey on camel, and Forrest soon realised his wisdom. A whole entry of Forrest's diary of this journey is devoted to the advantage of camels over horses. Forrest found that horses needed water every 12 hours if they were to survive and therefore, each day, Forrest and his men had to detour from their path and spend hours in the pursuit of water. By August of that year the party was in trouble. They were without water and feared turning back – as they could not guarantee finding water where they had previously. The only option was to keep moving forward. However, 1,500 km (950 miles) of arid, waterless expanse lay between them and the nearest settlement and the men and horses were in severe risk of dying from exhaustion and dehydration. But luck was on their side. It started to rain. This was considered something of a miracle in that part of the country and at that time of the year. The water holes filled and the men were able to carry on and achieve their goal. And so they did the unimaginable, and completed their horseback crossing.

The men discussed in this section are just a few of the explorers who survived the harshest of landscapes and numerous perils to contribute vital knowledge and understanding of the Australian interior territory. The esteemed naturalist and explorer, Alfred Russell Wallace, wrote in their praise, 'The work that has been already done in so inhospitable a country and so trying a climate is little less than marvellous; and the story of Australian exploration, with its episodes of heroism and martyrdom, affords a convincing proof of the undiminished energies of our countrymen in their southern home.'

Jungle

The dawning age of photography coincided with an era of increased European exploration and expansion in the tropical jungles of Africa and South America. Although South America had seen increasing contact with Europeans since Pizarro's conquest of the Inca empire from 1532 and in Africa the Portuguese navigator Vasco da Gama had reached the Cape of Good Hope in 1497, by the early 19th century, the interiors of those continents were still largely unknown to outsiders. In South America, the search for El Dorado, the 'Land of Gold' had pushed Spanish adventurers such as Cabeza de Vaca and Orellana (who traversed the Amazon east-to-west in 1541–42) inland, but the blanks on the map remained considerable. Similarly explorers such as Mungo Park, who explored the Niger in the late 18th century, revealed just how vast was the amount of territory still to be explored.

The African 'jungle' in the popular imagination constitutes merely one-tenth of the continent, yet this is the size of India. No living system on land is as diverse as the tropical rainforests of the world, with more than 8,000 plant species, 150 types of mammal, 600 species of bird and an almost infinite variety of insects. In fact these tropical havens contain almost half of the world's plants and animals.

One of the greatest explorers of the African jungle of this period, Henry Moreton Stanley, touched upon the great wonder of the tropical jungle in his book *Encounters on the Upper Congo*. Through his words, we sense the jungle as a feast for the senses and feel the same amazement that Stanley experienced in that pre-televisual era when such a landscape would have been totally alien and utterly new:

> 'One hears much about the "silence of the forest" – but the tropical forest is not so silent to the keen observer. The hum and the murmur of hundreds of busy insect tribes make populous the twilight shadows that reign under the primeval growth. I hear the grinding of millions of mandibles, the furious hiss of a tribe just alarmed or about to rush to battle, millions of tiny wings rustling through the nether air, the march of an insect tribe under the leaves, the startling leap of an awakened mantis, the chirp of some eager and garrulous cricket, the buzz of an ant-lion, the roar of a bullfrog … Silence is impossible in a tropical forest.'

EARLY EXPLORATION OF AFRICA

Tens of centuries before this account begins in the era of photography, Africa had been explored by outsiders in search of riches, new pastures or driven by religious belief. The Greek historian Herodotus recorded reports of an attempt in the sixth century BC by the Egyptian Pharaoh, Necho, to circumnavigate Africa. Certainly since the fifth century BC, Romans and Greeks, along with Arabs and ancient Egyptians, had explored the lower regions of the Nile for the purposes of trade. Arab traders crossed the Sahara and the Sudan region carrying salt, weapons, slaves, gold and ivory back and forth, leaving accounts of the area and its geography. A Greek expedition in AD 61–63 travelled up the Nile, probably further than any previous expeditions, and the participants became the last Europeans to do so until the 1830s. Arab geographers also contributed greatly to the knowledge of Africa; Abu Abdullah ash Sharif al-Idrisi (1100–65) wrote an account of the country around the Niger River, centuries before Mungo Park undertook two expeditions on the Niger between 1795 and 1806.

The Portuguese first circumnavigated and mapped the coast of Africa, with Vasco da Gama in 1498 establishing the sea route to Africa via the east coast. As a result, these coastal regions became European outposts, complete with missionaries. In particular, the Portuguese were in contact with Abyssinia, where Jesuit priests' attempts to convert the Emperor to their faith eventually resulted in their expulsion, but not before discovering the source of the Blue Nile in the early 17th century. Their claims were disputed by James Bruce, a Scot, who spent three years in the Abyssinian imperial court in 1798 and reached the source of the Blue Nile, declaring himself its true discoverer.

As a result, both the coasts and desert zone were fairly well mapped and explored by the 16th century, and it was the interior that remained a mystery. Stories of cannibals, savage tribes and strange animals were the common preconceptions of this part of the world to outsiders. Its unknown perils and startling differences were part of the reason the interior only became known at a much later date, but the dense forests, difficult terrain and the tropical climate and its resulting diseases played an equal role.

At this time, the main driver for European and Arabic exploration of Africa was the slave trade, but the end of the 18th century brought with it the ideals of the Enlightenment to Europe and therefore caused some to rethink the old preconceptions of Africa and the African people. As resistance to slavery grew and opportunities in the African continent became more imagined, filling in the 'great blanks on the map of Africa' took on a new purpose and a new meaning. In 1788, the Association for Promoting the Discovery of the Interior Parts of Africa – or the African Association – was formed, leading to developments in geography, the natural sciences and ethnography.

The Niger was one of the first regions to which the Association turned its attention, infused as it was with stories of the gold trade and the Nile.

below

Richard Burton was born in England in 1821, and spent many years abroad as a young boy, accompanying his parents on their travels throughout Europe. Burton was an eccentric, hugely intelligent and arrogant man, and claimed of his tutors whilst at Oxford that he was amongst 'grocers'. When expelled from Oxford for attending horse races, he rode his horse and carriage across the flowerbeds of the college and through the town, blowing a trumpet. Not only a great explorer, Burton was also a great scholar, ethnologist, translator, writer and linguist, learning around 25 languages in his lifetime. His taste for the Orient and all its exotic and sensual elements, as well as a reputation for homosexuality, placed him outside the mainstream of Victorian society.

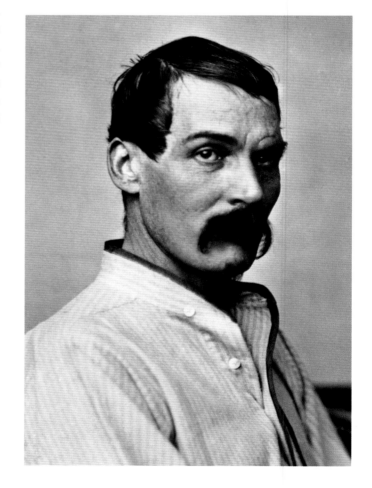

While he was later to be vindicated, John Hanning Speke's imprecise techniques and lack of thoroughness were fodder for the early scepticism of his Nile theories. He was the antithesis of Burton, reserved and aloof, and less concerned with being a geographer, surveyor and linguist and more with big game hunting and sportsmanship. He was a parody of the early British colonialist, being uninterested in local customs and cultures and with an innate sense of the white man's superiority over the African. In his *Journey of the Discovery of the Source of the Nile*, Speke reveals his rejection of native customs and insistence on his own ways: 'Now I had made up my mind never to sit upon the ground as the natives and Arabs are obliged to do, nor to make my obeisance in any other manner than is customary in England.'

Notable explorers of this region were Hugh Clapperton and Richard and John Lander; Richard became the first traveller to receive an award from the newly formed Geographical Society (later Royal). Further expeditions were undertaken by Dr William Baikie between 1854 and 1864, who translated the Book of Genesis into Hausa and pioneered the use of quinine for malaria. Henrich Barth, a German explorer, travelled 16,000 kms (10,000 miles) from Tripoli south to Lake Chad and on to Timbuktu and back again. Once the Niger had been mapped and explored more thoroughly, minds turned to the mystery of the Nile.

THE SOURCE OF THE NILE

'Egypt is a gift from the Nile' wrote the Greek historian Herodotus in the fifth century BC. Until the 19th century, it remained a mystery exactly how such a river could originate in an area which seemed never to receive rainfall and then flow through so many kilometres of desert to irrigate the country. Herodotus claimed that the Niger and the Nile were one and the same, and that the river flowed from West Africa across the Chad basin into Egypt. Seven centuries later, another Greek, Ptolemy, theorised that in fact there was a chain of high, snow-capped mountains from which three lakes gave birth to one tributary of the Nile, with the other tributary originating in the east. His theory was widely disparaged for centuries afterwards; the idea that snow-capped mountains could be found straddling the African equator was considered by many to be preposterous.

What, in fact, he had fairly correctly mapped was the basis of the Nile system: the Ruwenzori mountains (the *Lunae Montes* or the 'Mountains of the Moon'), its lakes, the White Nile (which flows from these lakes) and the Blue Nile (which originates in Ethiopia and which joins the White Nile to become the great Nile which flows through Egypt). Quite an incredible feat, considering that all his work was based on the reports and travels of others. The Blue Nile, shorter and less mysterious than the White, was discovered by Jesuit Missionaries in the 17th century. In comparison, the maze of lakes and rivers in central Africa made the discovery of the White Nile and its sources far more elusive. Indeed, geographical conditions made exploration of the area very difficult; a system of cataracts upstream of Aswan made the Nile unnavigable beyond that point. As a result, explorers tried instead to approach it on land from the east coast. Here again, the difficult climate and terrain made the journeys hazardous and long.

An Egyptian expedition in the 1820s, which travelled up to the junction of the White and Blue Niles, concluded that the Blue Nile was simply a tributary, but failed to go further south in search of the White Nile's sources. The first European reports of the White Nile system were in the 1840s, when the missionaries Ludwig Krapf, Johann Rebman and Johann Ebhardt told of great lakes and snow-capped mountains inland from the east coast – these mountains were to be Mount Kilimanjaro and Mount Kenya. The missionaries

above

Bombay was a member of Burton and Speke's expedition, but like most African expedition members who were fundamental to the success of an expedition, is relatively unknown. Porters and guides invariably travelled many more miles than their leaders, as experience with one explorer proved a good reference for another, and they were often keen to hire those who had experience in their predecessors' expeditions. For good guides and porters, exploration became a profession, whilst for others, the exhaustion and illnesses of long treks in the jungle meant death was a very real risk.

also reported a vast inland sea — what was to become Lakes Victoria, Albert and Tanganyika.

The source, or sources, of the White Nile was the great prize of African exploration at that time, and it was to take several incredible journeys during the mid- to late 1800s to establish which of the various reports, stories and theories approached the truth. The first great names of this period of exploration were Richard Francis Burton and John Hanning Speke. Both were officers of the British Indian Army, and had already distinguished themselves in similar ventures before this expedition. Burton had travelled throughout Arabia and India and Speke had mapped and travelled in the Himalayas and Tibet.

Burton and Speke had first travelled together on a previous African expedition in 1854 to discover the interior of Somaliland. During this journey, Burton became the first white man to enter and leave Harar alive, whilst Speke spent his time big-game hunting. The expedition was called off, however, after an attack by Somali tribesmen left one of the expedition's members dead and Burton and Speke wounded.

Two years later, Burton and Speke were hired by the Royal Geographical Society to solve the Nile mystery for the British Crown. Their expedition began in Zanzibar, recently declared independent of Oman and the gateway to East Africa at that time. The base of Arab ivory and slave traders, it was subject to growing British influence and was a place where explorers could hire porters and guides. Porters were fundamental to these expeditions, as pack animals were rarely used due to the dense jungle environment as well as the prevalence of the tsetse fly, which gave sleeping sickness. Burton and Speke were accompanied by around 100 porters, plus a 30-man armed escort, and carried various merchandise to give to those whose lands they would pass through.

On 13 February 1858, the two men were the first Europeans to sight Lake Tanganyika. Eight months of travelling had taken their toll, however, and Burton and Speke were so ill that they were forced to stop at Ujiji, a trading town on the shores of the lake. Speke was temporarily blind from ophthalmia and deaf from a beetle penetrating his ear, and Burton was virtually paralysed. Managing to explore the north side of the lake, they found that the Ruizizi River's low altitude meant that it was unlikely to be the source of the Nile and furthermore, it flowed into, rather than out of the lake. Despite not solving the mystery, Burton spoke of his willingness to endure the double of what they had suffered in discovering Lake Tanganyika in order to achieve a 'discovery' of similar importance. However, the journey was to mark the end of the two men's relationship. Following their return and recovery at Kazeh, they separated, and Speke headed north, following reports of another lake. This was to be Lake Victoria, and on 3 August 1858, based more on instinct than evidence, he renamed the source of the Nile after his Queen.

Speke proclaimed he had found the source of the Nile, but his haste to return and spread his news, with very little exploration of the region, led many to disparage his claims, not least Burton, who maintained that the prize lay toward Mount Kilimanjaro. The dispute divided geographical circles and when Speke returned to London and the Royal Geographical Society proclaiming his 'discovery', his new-found fame allowed him to fund a new expedition to collect further evidence.

Accompanied by a more pleasant and amenable traveller, James Augustus Grant, Speke headed for the shores of Lake Victoria from where they were the first Europeans to travel in the Bantu kingdoms. Here, Grant and Speke parted company, Grant heading north towards Bunyoro and Speke following the lake to the east. In July 1862 on the north side of the lake, Speke found the rapids from whence the Nile emerged, and proclaimed his theory had been proved. Although he had indeed found the point at which the Nile left this lake, he had not discovered its ultimate source, the source which fed the Lake.

Returning from their successful journey with supplies running short, Speke and Grant took a short cut and to their amazement bumped into an old friend, Samuel Baker, and his wife Florence. They too were hoping to take part in the Nile quest. A wealthy man, Baker had spent time in India and was also a keen big-game hunter. After his previous wife's death, Baker had been in Bulgaria hunting, and on the spur of the moment, while at a slave auction, bid for a beautiful Hungarian refugee: Florence Baker. Florence, praised for her *sang froid*, played an important role in their journey, Samuel declaring that he owed his success and life to her.

In *The Albert Nyanza*, Samuel Baker describes how Florence's blonde hair amazes the Africans: 'For the moment, I thought the hut was on fire, and I joined the crowd and arrived at the doorway, where I found a tremendous press to see some extraordinary sight. Everyone was squeezing for the best place; and, driving them to one side, I found the wonder that had excited their curiosity. The hut being very dark, my wife had employed her solitude during my conference with the natives in dressing her hair at the doorway, which, being very long and blonde, was suddenly noticed by some natives — a shout was given, the rush described had taken place, and the hut was literally mobbed by the crowd of savages eager to see the extraordinary novelty.'

The Bakers' journey began in Cairo in 1861, from where they took one year travelling to Khartoum, crossing the Nubian desert, learning Arabic, meeting with local chiefs and completing surveys of the many rivers which ran through the Ethiopian foothills. They met Speke and Grant at Gondoroko, and were disappointed at the news that Speke had won the prize. Yet Speke was generous with his information, and suggested that there might be another lake which formed part of the Nile system, providing them with maps and advice from his own expeditions.

This lake was Luta Nzigé, or Lake Albert, renamed after Queen Victoria's husband. Yet there remained confusion as to how many sources in fact there were, as the Bakers returned to Cairo without fully exploring and mapping the Lake and its connection with Lake Victoria. Samuel Baker was to write an account of his travels entitled *The Albert Nyanza* in which his eye for superficial detail contrasted sharply with his descriptions of the people of the lakes, whom he whitewashed as barbaric and wild.

During this time, Speke and Grant were on their way home, claiming they had settled once and for all the question of the source of the Nile. They returned to England as heroes, yet there was still a contingency of unbelievers who wanted more evidence, among them, of course, Burton. The British Association for the Advancement of Science arranged a public meeting between the two men— yet that very day, Speke died in a shooting accident, considered by some to have been suicide. The meeting was quickly reorganised, to consist of a talk by Burton followed by a talk by David Livingstone, who had just returned from his expedition to the Zambezi, and considered an expert on the region. Livingstone was requested to undertake another expedition to provide more evidence to solve the dispute.

Speke describes his surprise meeting with Samuel Baker: 'Walking down the bank of the river — where a line of vessels was moored, ... we saw hurrying towards us the form of an Englishman, who, for a moment, we believed was Simon Pure; but the next moment my old friend Baker, famed for his sports in Ceylon, seized me by the hand.'

LIVINGSTONE

Livingstone had already travelled extensively in Africa before being tasked with his Nile mission. He first set sail to the continent in 1840 at the age of 27, arriving at Kuruman, 804 kms (500 miles) north of the Cape, to work at the mission of Robert Moffat, whose daughter Mary he married. The couple moved frequently, trying to avoid the violent land disputes between the Boers and the local peoples. Livingstone's sympathetic manner with the natives and his proficiency as a doctor won him respect. It is while at one of these missions in Mabotsa that one of his famous incidents took place. Livingstone took it upon himself to rid the valley of its infestation of lions and having heard that killing one lion would cause the rest to leave the area, he set out hunting. After shooting one lion, he was reloading his gun when the lion sprang at him and shook him, crushing his left arm. The lion attacked two further men in the party before dropping dead from the bullet. Livingstone never regained the full use and power of his arm.

In 1849, Livingstone and his sponsor and friend William Cotton Oswell became the first Europeans to cross the Kalahari and set eyes on Lake Ngami. This experience fuelled Livingstone's imagination for other, more ambitious expeditions. In 1851 he travelled to the Cuando and Zambezi rivers, beyond which

above

David Livingstone began his life near Glasgow in Scotland in 1813 and at ten, he was sent to work in a cotton factory, studying each night at night school. Rising to cotton-spinner, he earnt enough to study medicine, Greek and theology in Glasgow and London. His original intention was to become a missionary in China, but the onset of the Opium Wars closed off the country to him. In 1839, Livingstone met Dr Robert Moffat, who told of the 'smoke of a thousand villages, where no missionary has ever been' in Africa. Livingstone's fate was sealed. He spent the majority of his life in Africa, and remains one of the continent's most famous explorers.

lay vast uncharted territory. Although others are claimed to have reached the Zambezi and crossed this territory before Livingstone, his extensive and detailed notes and maps meant that it was Livingstone who brought this geographical knowledge to the world.

Not driven simply by his desire to spread the gospel, Livingstone was also appalled by the prevalence of the slave trade. Though the Act of Abolition had reduced some of the slave traffic on the west coast, it persisted there and in other areas. Livingstone's aim was to fight slavery by encouraging an 'honest' trade of industry and commerce to develop amongst the local peoples. However, this could not happen without an effective and rapid route into the interior to facilitate it.

At this stage, his family was still with him, and Livingstone decided – whether for their own health and safety or for his own freedom of movement – to send them back to England. He set off again in 1853, travelling westerly with a small number of African men by boat and ox, collecting specimens of medicinal plants and making use of a magic lantern, which showed scenes from the Bible, to communicate with people. By May 1854 the party had reached the Atlantic Ocean and after a period of recuperation, they travelled back; in all, they had travelled over 4,000 kms (2,500 miles). It was this factor that forced him to rethink; this was too long and complicated a route to serve his aim of opening up the interior. Another journey, this time eastward, brought him upon the 'Mosioatunya' falls, or 'the smoke which thunders', which he renamed the Victoria Falls. Livingstone, exhausted, arrived in Quelimane, Mozambique on a litter, becoming the first European to cross Africa from west to east. There, he received a letter requesting his severance from the London Missionary Society, who were displeased with his change of emphasis from missionary work to exploration.

Livingstone returned to England in 1856, after 16 years away, to a great reception, and his account of his travels, *Missionary Travels and Researches in South Africa*, became a bestseller. He used his new-found celebrity to drum up awareness of, and support against, the reality of slavery.

Livingstone led another expedition in 1858 to open up the Zambezi as a route into the interior, sponsored by the Foreign Office and the RGS. Accompanied by six British men and around 60 porters, he 'discovered' Lake Nyasa and the courses of two rivers, the Shire and Rovuma, and established a mission on the former river. Such a mission in the interior had been one of his dreams, but lasted only briefly up to the death of Bishop Mackenzie in 1862. That year, his wife rejoined him, but within months she had also succumbed to a fever. In 18 years of marriage, they had spent less than half that time together. Coupled with his inability to lead a team, his boat proving a hindrance, and faced with the reality that the Zambezi was unnavigable across a certain stretch of its waters, the expedition was a failure.

right

Henry Morton Stanley was an illegitimate child born in Denbigh, North Wales, in 1841. At the age of five, he was assigned to a workhouse from where he eventually ran away to sea and America, where he was to make his living as a reporter. He was known as Bula Matari, 'Breaker of Bones', by some Africans because of his single-mindedness and fierce determination. He is credited with finally solving the mystery of the Nile sources, confirming Speke's earlier contentious claims.

right

The site where Livingstone's heart lies buried at Chitambo, Lake Bangweulu in Zambia. The tree has now been cut down, but the part with this inscription is held at the Royal Geographical Society in London. His companions carried his embalmed body and his journals 2,250 kms (1,400 miles) to the coast from where he was carried back to London and buried in Westminster Abbey. Chuma and Susi, his captain and headman, travelled to England, but arrived too late for the funeral.

Livingstone continued to fight against the slave trade and lobbied the Portuguese king into agreeing to cooperate. However, Portuguese officers ignored his directions and in 1864 the expedition was recalled as a result of both Portuguese pressure and financial considerations.

LIVINGSTONE AND THE NILE

Shortly after returning to Britain, Livingstone set out again to play his part in the debate that was then raging over the mystery of the Nile. Following the death of Speke, Livingstone was hired by the RGS to settle the matter once and for all. Landing at the mouth of the Rovuma, in Portuguese territory, his party travelled north-west via Lake Nyasa to Lake Tanganyika, discovering Lake Mweru and its effluent, the Lualaba River, which he believed was the Nile. Unfriendly Arab traders thwarted him in his attempt to follow the Lualaba downstream, and he returned to Ujiji weakened, both mentally and physically. Livingstone had spent six years on this particular journey, a journey he expected to have completed much more rapidly. By 1871 Europe had not heard from him for some time and rumours of his death had started to circulate.

Such was the interest in Livingstone's whereabouts that Henry Morton Stanley, a young Welsh-born American journalist, travelled to Africa in search of him. Sent there by his employer James Gordon Bennett, the proprietor of the *New York Herald*, Stanley was effectively given a blank cheque to get the story, a story that would bring enormous publicity to the newspaper. The legendary meeting between Livingstone and Stanley took place on the shores of Lake Tanganyika, and Stanley's famous words came about as a result of his inability to judge how to greet such a man, in such a situation, and in such a place:

below

Henry Morton Stanley is shown pictured in Zanzibar. The island kingdom had become a centre for trade and discovery in the region – including the slave trade. It also became the base for many of the early expeditions that explored the African continent. Livingstone's House can still be seen in Stone Town. When Burton and Speke set off to solve the mystery of the source of the Nile in 1857 they too made Zanzibar their staging post.

below right

The Emin Pasha relief expedition was intended as an imperial venture, but it also revealed the Ituri Forest, Lake Edward and the Ruwenzoir massif. Here, local traders are shown on Lake Edward.

'I would have run to him, only I was a coward in the presence of such a mob – would have embraced him, only, he being an Englishman, I did not know how he would receive me; so I did what cowardice and false pride suggested was the best thing – walked deliberately to him, took off my hat and said…'

'Dr Livingstone, I presume?' was his greeting to a tired and jaded man. Yet, in Stanley's presence, Livingstone rediscovered his energy. They explored the northern end of Lake Tanganyika, establishing that what was thought to be the Nile was in fact the Ruizizi, and it flowed into the lake rather than out of it. Livingstone again turned to the Lualaba, convinced that at its source were the four fountains that Herodotus had claimed and that it was a headwater of the Nile. Disregarding Stanley's attempts to make him return to England because of his ill-health, Livingstone left Stanley at Kazeh in March 1872 and travelled to Lake Bangweulu to try to prove his theory. Increasingly ill and suffering repeated haemorrhages, Livingstone died in May 1873, as he knelt at the foot of his bed. Chuma and Susi, his devoted companions, buried his heart and organs by a tree on which they engraved his name. Then, embalmed in salt and alcohol, he was carried to Zanzibar and taken home to be buried in Westminster Abbey the following year.

Undeterred, Stanley took on the task of navigating the Lualaba, financed now by the proprietors of the *New York Herald* and *The Daily Telegraph*. His route passed through Lake Victoria and the Kingdom of Buganda — which Speke and Grant had visited a decade previously. They then travelled south to Lake Tanganyika, and the circumnavigation of the lake proved it had no relationship with the Nile. The only outlet was the Lukuga River, which fed the Lualaba. On his expedition to follow the course of this river, Stanley's party fought 34 battles with people on the banks of the river or in canoes, and navigated rapids and falls. At the final test, the Livingstone (or Stanley) Falls, where the river descends 300m (984 ft) over 32 cataracts, the last European man in the party (save Stanley) was drowned. One thousand days after the journey began, 114 men

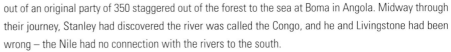

out of an original party of 350 staggered out of the forest to the sea at Boma in Angola. Midway through their journey, Stanley had discovered the river was called the Congo, and he and Livingstone had been wrong – the Nile had no connection with the rivers to the south.

Stanley's Congo expedition, however, had not diminished his interest in the area, and he returned to England to generate support for the development of the region. With the Conservative administration uninterested in his propositions, Stanley was approached by King Leopold II of Belgium who founded the Association Internationale Africaine as a basis for his imperial designs on West Africa. By July 1879 Stanley was back in the Congo basin, building a railway and founding Leopoldville, which later became Kinshasa. His arrival beat the French who, led by Count Pierre Savorgnan de Brazza, were forced to the other bank and created Brazzaville, now capital city of the Congo.

Stanley was to return once more to the Congo on the Emin Pasha relief expedition in 1887. Emin was a German naturalist employed by the Egyptian government in their short-lived empire in southern Sudan. He had become cut off near Lake Albert during a Madhist uprising in 1881. The relief party came from the west coast via the Congo and the Aruwimi River rather than the more well-trodden road from the east, struggling through some of the densest forest on earth for five months. The forests were also home to tribes of pygmies who attacked them with poisoned arrows; as a result of these attacks and the harsh conditions, the death toll was extremely high. Emin Pasha, who was unconcerned at the position he was in, needed some persuasion to leave. He later returned and was killed there. It was during this return journey that Stanley glimpsed the Ruwenzori or the 'Mountains of the Moon', the legendary peaks that Ptolemy had written of so many centuries previously. His party traced its way around the mountains and discovered how their water fed the Semliki River and, henceforth, Lake Albert. The final piece of the

right

Stanley: 'Ruwenzori has been visible the last three days. That snow-covered range has been a most attractive and beautiful sight – pure, dazzling, varying in colours with the hours, with infinite depth of opaline blue all round it, until the sun set and dark night covered the earth … We have not much to boast of … the ancient travellers, geographers and authors had a very fair idea of whence the Nile issued … had heard of the Lunae Montes, and the triple lakes, and of the springs which gave birth to the famous river of Egypt.'

mystery had been put in place – the geography of the Nile sources was finally completed.

The race to claim territories in the Congo basin was the beginning of what came to be known as 'The Scramble'. In 1884, the Berlin Conference had been called to assess and even check the speed at which Europe was claiming Africa but, increasingly, exploratory motives were now much more based on political, rather than inquisitive and geographical desires. The Marchand Mission, for example, was a French attempt to prevent the British from claiming the Congo–Nile watershed, and Stanley attempted to win the valuable and respected service of Emin Pasha for the British. Despite Stanley's rescue, Pasha instead offered his services to Germany and was given the task of securing the territories south of and along Lake Victoria and up to Lake Albert.

SCHWEINFURTH AND THOMSON

Aside from the Nile quest, the African jungle was further explored during and after this period by Schweinfurth, Thomson and Kingsley. Between 1869 and 1871, Georg August Schweinfurth, a German botanist, explored more thoroughly the Bahr el Ghazl, the equatorial region south-west of the Nile. Primarily interested in hunting for plants, Schweinfurth was also fascinated, as were so many at that time, by stories of cannibals and pygmies. Though unknown to Europeans, the area was already well travelled by slave and ivory traders and was criss-crossed with their stations. On foot, he travelled through the jungle with these traders for protection, as their activity had made the native tribes highly suspicious and aggressive towards outsiders.

above

In 1897, French Captain Jean-Baptiste Marchand was in charge of an expedition aiming to explore the virtually unknown area of the Nile–Congo watershed. His objective was to establish a French presence from Fashoda in the east, 650 kms (410 miles) south of Khartoum to Libreville in the west, cutting off the British advance south. Upon reaching Fashoda, however, they were met by 20,000 of Kitchener's men who forced them to retreat. Marchand is pictured here in the centre.

Accompanying the ivory traders, Schweinfurth ventured into areas reputed to be inhabited by cannibals, and became the first European to stand on the bank of the Uele River and the first European to meet the Akka pygmies. In exchange for his dog, he was given one pygmy, whom he hoped to take back to Germany with him, but Tikkitikki (as he had named him), reportedly died from overeating. Schweinfurth spent two and a half years in this region, from which he was to write *The Heart of Africa*, but unfortunately, on his return journey, all of his specimens and notes were lost in a camp fire. Without his tools, Schweinfurth apparently counted his steps back to Khartoum – all 1.25 million of them. Schweinfurth's health was to continue into his nineties and he went on to travel to Lebanon and Yemen and became the first European to explore parts of the Libyan Desert.

In 1882, while in Cairo, Schweinfurth received a visitor named Joseph Thomson. Thomson was a young geologist from Scotland, who had joined an RGS expedition to explore further the central African lakes. After the early death of the expedition's commander and as second-in-command, he took the lead. He took to entertaining the native people by removing his false teeth and dropping fruit salts which fizzed and popped in water. His first expedition to the north end of Lake Nyasa and further exploration of Lake Tanganyika proved

successful, and he was consequently requested to head another expedition.

The expedition's aim was to explore a possible route across Masai country from Mombasa to the northern shores of Lake Victoria, the most direct route from the coast to the lake. The Masai country was reportedly very hostile, and at that time had not been significantly travelled by European explorers. It was while on this expedition that Thomson sighted the gazelle that was named in his honour – Thomson's Gazelle, and travelled north up the Rift Valley and 'discovered' Thomson's Falls (Nyahururu). He also climbed the extinct volcano Longonot to look down into its cauldron. Thomson was later to work for the British South Africa Company, negotiating political and mining rights in today's Zambia. He put his success down to his prudence, saying, 'He who goes slowly goes safely; he who goes safely goes far', but was to die at an early age back in England.

MARY HENRIETTA KINGSLEY

African exploration was clearly not for the faint-hearted. The list of African explorers is dominated by men, which makes the work of Mary Henrietta Kingsley even more remarkable. Explorer, writer and ethnologist, Kingsley was a critic of mainstream European colonialism and was influential through her enlightened opinions of the validity of African culture and customs and the need for a 'civilised' European presence in Africa.

Born in London in 1862, Kingsley lived a sheltered life at home, and with a limited education – typical of girls of that time – she made use of her father's extensive library, while he was on frequent trips abroad. She lived a rather parochial life until the age of 30, when both her parents died. Kingsley had spent much of the last few years before his death assisting her father with his life's work – a comparative study of sacrificial rites around the world – one he was never able to finish. With her brother leaving for China, Kingsley was suddenly free to pursue her own interests, and she decided to try to complete her father's work, and collect exhibits for the British Museum at the same time. After only one trip abroad, to the Canary Islands, she set sail for Equatorial Africa in 1893.

With only modest funds to support her, Kingsley travelled simply. She arrived with £300, a portmanteau, collecting boxes and not a word of French or any African languages. Accompanied by just

above left

Mr Marnewick, a member of Laurens Van der Post's expedition to the Kalahari, is shown here in 1955 with two pygmies. The pygmy to Marnewick's immediate right is believed to be around 60 years old. Laurens Van der Post was born in 1906 in South Africa and spent several years living with the bushmen of the Kalahari. A great writer and thinker, Van der Post was a very close friend of Jung's for two decades, and used his experiences in the Kalahari to reflect on his conception of the modern man. Of the Kalahari people he said, 'The one outstanding characteristic of these people (San people of the Kalahari) as I knew them, and which distinguished them from us was that wherever they went, they felt they were known. The staggering loss of identity and meaning that we, in the modern world experience, was unknown to them'.

above

Joseph Thomson travelled through the Masai country, renowned for its fierce warriors who were hostile towards traders passing through their land. Despite frequent skirmishes with the Masai, Thomson reportedly never killed a native. Though informal and entertaining, Thomson was known as a careful and prudent traveller. When asked what the most hazardous part of his expedition was, he replied, 'Crossing Piccadilly Circus'.

opposite
The Fan people, who Kingsley spent considerable time living with and studying, were cannibals. In her classic book, *Travels in West Africa*, she describes coming across human remains in a Fan town: 'Waking up, I noticed the smell in the hut was violent … and it had an unmistakable organic origin … I investigated, and tracked it to those bags … I then shook its contents out into my hat, for fear of losing anything of value. They were a human hand, three big toes, four eyes, two ears, and other portions of the human frame … I subsequently learnt that although the Fans will eat their fellow friendly tribesfolk, yet they like to keep a little something belonging to them as a memento. This touching trait I learnt from Wiki; and although it's to their credit, under the circumstances, it's still an unpleasant practice when they hang the remains in the bedroom you occupy, particularly if the bereavement in your host's family has been recent.'

above
Mrs E Barton Worthington with two Kenyans using a plane table on the shore of Lake Rudolph. Lake Rudolph is now called Lake Turkana, or sometimes the Jade Sea, and is located in the Rift Valley, Kenya. This remote lake is half the size of England.

below
'I would much sooner wade through a swamp up to my neck or climb the peak of the Cameroon, than go through the treadmill life.' Mary Kingsley lived her life true to these ideals.

a few porters, she refused to be carried, ate local foods, slept under the stars and learned how to manage a canoe single-handedly. She must have looked most incongruous in that setting – unwilling as she was to 'go to Africa in things you would be ashamed of at home'. Effectively, this meant travelling in long, black, tight-waisted skirts and high-necked blouses. However, her particular dress was to save her life at one stage when she fell into a game-pit, her many petticoats protecting her from the stakes.

On the search for 'fish and fetish', as she termed her journey, she collected freshwater fish specimens for the British Museum and information for herself on African religions, trading rum, tobacco, cloth and fishhooks in exchange. She delivered 65 species of fish to the British Museum on her return – three of which were new to science and were subsequently named after her.

Kingsley's voyages took her to exploring the coast between Senegal and Angola, Kabinda, Fernando Po, the Congo, the Ogowé River, and she spent a considerable time living among the Fang people of Gabon, whom she renamed Fan to lessen their infamous reputation. Despite their reputation and their cannibalism, Kingsley's writings of this experience show that she was ahead of her time. Of her preconceptions of the Fan, she says:

'One by one I took my old ideas derived from books and thoughts based on imperfect knowledge and weighed them against the real life around me, and found them either worthless or wanting.'

On her return to London in 1895 after her two voyages, Kingsley wrote her classic book *Travels in West Africa*, which was reprinted four times in its first year of publication and which was quickly followed by a second volume, *West African Studies*. A master of understatement, she described being covered with a collar of leeches after one particular swim, and discovering human body parts in the tent she slept in. She also achieved her ambition of climbing Mount Cameroon by a route never before attempted, and in typical fashion, left her visiting card under a stone at the summit.

Kingsley's experiences later led her to be considered an authority on the African world and she had the respect of Joseph Chamberlain, the Minister for the Colonies, as well as Stanley and Rudyard Kipling. Kingsley had planned a third expedition to the region, but instead travelled to South Africa where she nursed soldiers in the Boer War. At the young age of 39, she died of a tropical disease, and the Mary Kingsley Society – which was to become the African Society – was founded in her honour.

right

Gustav Nachtigal (1834–85), a German explorer, travelled from Borno in 1869 on a five-year voyage through Tibetsi and Borkou (previously unknown to Europeans), Chad, the Sudan and down the Nile to Khartoum. His travels were described in his book *Sahara and Sudan*. He became the Consul-General for Germany in Tunis until 1884 after which he travelled as part of 'The Scramble' to claim West African territories for Germany. He managed to annexe Togo and Cameroon before dying on his return journey.

far right

In the wake of the explorers came the tourists. Thomas Cook, pictured here, organised his first tour of Egypt and the Nile as early as 1869. So well-established was the company in Africa, that in 1884 the British government asked Thomas Cook to organise the logistics for the expedition to relieve Lord Gordon in Khartoum. Six thousand railway trucks, 27 river steamers and 600 boats were needed to haul the supplies and 5,000 Egyptians employed in the endeavour.

right

Carl and Mary Leonore Jobe Akeley are pictured here around 1926 in the Lukenia Hills in Kenya. Akeley was collecting specimens for the Hall of African Mammals he had been hired to create for the American Museum of Natural History in New York. Mary became Carl Akeley's second wife in 1924. Mary had already proved herself as a traveller and explorer, becoming the first white woman to witness the gift-exchange ceremony between native Indians in the Canadian Rockies, in recognition of which she was given the name Dene-Sczaki or 'man-woman' by the tribe. Carl travelled to Africa with both his wives at different times. He and his first wife, Delia Julia Denning Akeley, were to divorce soon after the end of World War I, and Delia returned to Africa and continued to collect specimens, now for the Brooklyn Museum of Art. Delia became the first woman to cross Africa from coast to coast.

SOUTH AMERICA

It is the name of Christopher Columbus which is most closely linked with the discovery of the Americas. Although Genoese, he was unable to convince his own country to fund him on his journey, and instead received funding from the Spanish, under whose flag he travelled. He made three separate voyages to various ports in the West Indies and the mouth of the Orinoco River in Brazil, but always remained convinced he had found the East Indies, the islands off the coast of China. It was, instead, Amerigo Vespucci, whose own journeys were contemporaneous with Columbus's final voyages, who gave his name to the continent. The Spanish conquistadors, who followed in their wake changed the face of the continent which had previously been dominated by the great civilisations of the Incas and Aztecs.

In the second half of the 18th century, South America's coastline was being mapped and explored by seafarers such as Anson, Cook, Malaspina and Fitzroy, whose naturalist, Charles Darwin, was to use his voyage's discoveries to revolutionise our conceptions of creation and the variety of the natural world. Exploration of the interior of the continent was principally driven by intrepid explorers with scientific aims, and many of the names associated with it are those of scientists, botanists and such like.

Alfred Russell Wallace and Henry Walter Bates arrived in Brazil together in 1848. Wallace was Bates's English master at his school in Leicester, and there they developed a close friendship after discovering a mutual interest in entomology and remote places. Books such as W. H. Edwards's *Voyage Up the River Amazon, Including a Residence at Para* and an exhibition of Amazonian butterflies at the British Museum all conspired to direct Bates's fate. In 1848, while working as an office clerk in Stoke-on-Trent, he accepted Wallace's invitation to join him in collecting butterfly specimens in the Amazon.

Arriving at Santarem in 1850, they were to spend only two years together before they parted. Wallace travelled up the Rio Negro, where his health deteriorated, and in 1852 he set sail for England. The ship in which he was travelling caught fire, however, and his six years of collections were lost. He did manage

above

Home to an estimated 3,000 species, the Amazon has the greatest diversity of freshwater fish of any river basin in the world. Traditionally the most feared by river explorers was the piranha, also known as the caribe. Although its reputation for ferocity may be somewhat exaggerated, its rows of serrated teeth give the fish a very threatening aspect. Packs of piranhas certainly do prey on other fish, including large ones, but attacks on humans allegedly ascribed to them are most probably fictitious.

to salvage something from the ruins, and wrote from memory an entire book on Amazonian palms and a more general book entitled *A Narrative of Travels on the Amazon and Rio Negro*.

Bates was to remain in Amazonia for a further seven years, during which time he collected around 14,000 species of insects – 8,000 of which were new to science – and travelled into Upper Amazonia. While there, he received correspondence from Wallace, now in the Malay Archipelago, who was beginning to put down and establish his ideas on natural selection. Bates was taken aback by the direction that his friend's ideas – ones they had once formulated together – were beginning to take, but was converted with the later publication of Darwin's *On the Origin of Species*.

Back in England, and with these ideas in his mind, Bates began to sort and make sense of his collection. One of the common Amazonian butterflies he examined was strongly smelling and unpalatable to predators due to the chemicals absorbed by the caterpillars from the Passionflower vines they fed upon. He also noticed a very similar-looking type, but these were not unpalatable. And so, indistinguishable to birds, they escaped predation by their likeness to the unpalatable variety. Bates was to discover many more specimens exhibiting this same characteristic, and it was to become known as Batesian mimicry. Darwin was impressed with the paper and its findings, as it offered further evidence to support his controversial theory.

Darwin encouraged Bates to write a memoir of his time on the Amazon, and Bates duly responded with *The Naturalist on the River Amazon*. The book not only concerned itself with butterflies and science, it also observed the fascinating customs and cultures of the Amazonians he came into contact with. *The Naturalist* was widely praised and reprinted several times and in several languages, a fitting recompense to Bates's work that netted him very little from the sale of his butterflies. Bates went on to become the first paid secretary of the Royal Geographical Society after missing out on a coveted post in the Zoology department of the British Library. Through his position, he was later to supervise the publication of several important books, including P. E. Warburton's *Journey Across the Western Interior of Australia*. He was also to receive the Brazilian Order of the Rose, an honour very rarely bestowed on foreigners.

MATO GROSSO

The Mato Grosso state of Brazil is right in the heart of the South American continent, and its capital city, Cuiabá, is the only large city in this remote area. It is here that President Theodore Roosevelt, who had just lost the 1912 election, travelled to hunt, explore and collect specimens. Roosevelt's 1909 safari, which took him to the jungles of Kenya, Uganda, Tanganyika and Nyasaland, had whetted his appetite. Whilst in Brazil, he was told of the River of Doubt by the Brazilian Minister of Foreign Affairs, so called as it was uncharted and its origin unknown. Also on his advice, Roosevelt hired Colonel Candido Mariano da Silva Rondon to help him explore it.

Setting off on 9 December, 1913, Roosevelt's party undertook a 1,448 kms trek (900 miles) to reach the headwaters of the river. Their party, including his son, Kermit, a naturalist, a physician and a Brazilian Lieutenant were transported down the river by skilled canoeists in dugout canoes. The river, criss-crossed

left

Theodore Roosevelt was the 26th and youngest President of the United States, taking office from 1901 to 1909. He was also Vice President, Governor of New York, Police Commissioner of New York City, Assistant Secretary of the Navy, a world's authority on large American mammals, President of the American Historical Association, one of the first fifteen to be elected to the American Academy of Arts and Letters and the founder of the National Collegiate Athletic Association and the Long Island Bird Club, amongst others. During his time in the White House he designated 150 National Forests, the first 51 Federal Bird Reservations, 5 National Parks, the first 18 National Monuments, the first 4 National Game Preserves, and the first 21 Reclamation Projects. All in all, he covered almost 220 million acres with federal protection. Professor Brander Matthews of Columbia University said of him: 'The more closely we scrutinize Theodore Roosevelt's life and the more carefully we consider his many ventures in totally different fields of human activity, the less likely we are to challenge the assertion that his was the most interesting career ever vouchsafed to any American.'

above
'On 27 February, 1914, shortly after midday, we started down the River of Doubt into the unknown. We were quite uncertain whether after a week we should find ourselves in the Gy-Parana, or after six weeks in the Madeira, or after three months we knew not where. That was why the river was rightly christened the Duvida ... The paddlers were a strapping set. They were expert river-men and men of the forest, skilled veterans in wilderness work. They were lithe as panthers and brawny as bears. They swam like water-dogs. They were equally at home with pole and paddle, with axe and machete; and one was a good cook and others were good men around camp. They looked like pirates in the pictures of Howard Pyle or Maxfield Parrish; one or two of them were pirates, and one worse than a pirate; but most of them were hard-working, willing and cheerful.'
Roosevelt, *Through the Brazilian Wilderness*

above right
Fawcett originally went to South America to undertake mapping and surveying projects for the Royal Geographical Society. South America, in particular the jungle of Bolivia and Brazil, was a vast, untapped source of rubber but also a vast uncharted wilderness. Borders were needed, so it was said, to prevent disputes over the potential economic benefit of the rubber yield. Since a third-party surveyor was needed, the job was taken on by the British, and Percy Fawcett in particular.

with dangerous rapids, obstacles and falls, claimed a life and scattered their food supplies. Its increasing violence and their dwindling supplies forced the men to travel in part by foot and to hunt and search for food in the form of monkey meat, brazil nuts and piranha fish.

Roosevelt and his party reached the end of the River of Doubt in 1913, having collected over 2,000 species of birds and 500 mammals. They had also collected vital information, which enabled parts of the interior of Brazil to be mapped for the first time. Considered a great success, the river was renamed Roosevelt River by the Brazilian Government, but Roosevelt's own personal reward was not as great. He later claimed, 'The Brazilian wilderness stole away 10 years of my life.' He was to die just 10 years later from ill-health and recurring malaria.

Rondon went on to be a founder of the Indian Protection Service (SPI), which still campaigns for the humane treatment and rights of the indigenous peoples of the Amazon. During his expeditions he had a strict policy of non-violence, and his motto 'Die if necessary, but never kill!' became the motto of the SPI. He was later to be nominated for the Nobel Peace Prize.

The Mato Grosso area was further explored by a British army colonel named Percy Fawcett, who undertook mapping surveys for the RGS on the Brazilian/Bolivian border. Fawcett, who was born in Devon in 1867, had previously served in Ceylon and in the secret service in North Africa but had taken up surveying in the hope it would lead to adventure. It was to do exactly that. In 1906 he travelled to La Paz in Bolivia, and began his journey into the jungle via a 5,700 m (19,000 ft) pass. Tested not only by the high altitudes, tropical diseases, dangerous animals and challenging terrain, Fawcett was also to come into close contact with defensive or hostile tribes. At one point, faced with an onslaught of poisonous arrows, he is said to have instructed one of his group to play the tunes of *A Bicycle Made for Two* and *Onward, Christian Soldiers* on his accordion, a plan which duly worked and pacified the Indians.

Fawcett was to map the River Verde and discover its source before returning to England to serve in World War I, but he was quickly to return to the jungle. During the years he spent mapping the area, he became steadily more fascinated by stories of a ruined city deep in the jungle. Wanting to take a small, reliable group, he employed his son, his friend and three assistants to join him, and in April 1925 set out, leaving instructions that if they were not to return, no rescue party was to be launched. At the end of May, his wife received a message from Fawcett, saying that they were beginning to enter unexplored territory and were leaving their three assistants behind. They have never been heard of since.

In the following years, despite Fawcett's instructions, several rescue expeditions were attempted. In 1928, an American press syndicate financed an expedition and returned with various trinkets, which may have belonged to the party. Various stories claimed that white men had been killed or captured by Indians;

above
Mato Grosso, which means 'thick wood', was where Fawcett travelled and eventually disappeared. The northern part of this region leads into the Amazon jungle where, during Fawcett's time, the huge untapped rubber supply was beginning to be realised.

above right
'Are these Missing Briton's Remains?' The skull and bones believed to be Colonel Fawcett's are shown here to Brazilian reporters by Orlando Vilasboas, leader of an expedition to discover Fawcett's fate in 1951. They were later found not to be Fawcett's remains and his disappearance still remains a mystery.

right
Hiram Bingham was born in 1875 in Honolulu, the son and grandson of missionaries. After achieving his PhD from Harvard in 1905, Bingham followed the route that the explorer Bolivar had taken in 1819 from which he wrote *Journal of an Expedition across Venezuela and Colombia*, and then took a journey following the Spanish trade route from Buenos Aires to Lima, Peru, which led to *Across South America*. He was a senator for eight years. He married in 1900 and had seven sons.

a Swiss explorer claimed to have met an English colonel and a missionary claimed to have seen a white child fathered by Fawcett. Twenty-five years later, a Brazilian anthropologist received bones that were claimed to be Fawcett's; they were transferred to England where examinations proved that was not the case. Even as late as 1996, an expedition was put together to find traces of him, but defensive Indians stopped the group, detaining and threatening them. His fate remains a mystery to this day.

MACHU PICCHU

To the west of the Brazilian and Bolivian jungle lie the long mountain chain of the Andes which, until the arrival of the Conquistadores, had been the realm of the Inca empire. At the beginning of the 16th century when the

Conquistadores arrived, there were 15 million Incas living in the Andes of South America, an empire that stretched around 4,800 kms (3,000 miles) from north to south. The Conquistadores ransacked the empire in search of its gold and mineral riches. Centuries later, the Andes also proved irresistible to Hiram Bingham, a lecturer in Latin American History at Yale and Harvard, who was fascinated by the glorious past of the Incas in their mountain kingdom. He undertook various journeys in South America in the search for the lost Inca cities of Vilcabamba and Vitcos, culminating in 1911 with his 'discovery' of Vilcabamba, the ruins of which he called Machu Picchu.

In *Inca Land: Explorations in the Highlands of Peru* Bingham describes the scene in the Urubamba Valley from where upon one of its mountains he uncovered Machu Picchu. His love for and appreciation of this region is expressed here in such a way that explains the consistent and eternal fascination with the jungle, whether

Inca legends tell of their civilisation arising from survivors of an epic flood from which they escaped by climbing up onto high peaks. The parallel with the Bible is striking, and it is perhaps peaks such as Machu Picchu that would have been where they would have found refuge. The Inca civilisation was incredibly rich, a richness that was plundered with the arrival of the Conquistadors in the 16th century. At the time of the Conquistadors' arrival, the Incas' Andes road network stretched 40,233 kms (25,000 miles) from Colombia to northern Chile. The study and understanding of this incredible culture is limited by the absence of written records. Some claim that the Incas did not write, whilst others have deciphered some of the symbols and engravings found on buildings. Here Bingham is seen taking survey readings.

below

Henry Savage Landor was an artist and explorer, whose adventures included an attempt to penetrate Tibet in 1897, which ended in his capture by a local Tibetan ruler, to exploration of the Kurile Islands north of Japan and extensive scientific surveys of South America between 1903 and 1912. He charted the course of the Amazon river and ventured through Ecuador, Peru, Bolivia, Chile, Argentina and Uruguay, recording the landscapes and local cultures. He published an account of these voyages in 1913 as *Across Unknown South America*.

it be in Africa or South America:

'In the variety of its charms and the power of its spell, I know of no place in the world which can compare with it. Not only has it great snow peaks looming above the clouds more than two miles overhead; gigantic precipices of many-coloured granite rising sheer for thousands of feet above the foaming, glistening, roaring rapids; it has also, in striking contrast, orchids and tree ferns, the delectable beauty of luxurious vegetation, and the mysterious witchery of the jungle.'

Bingham went on to discover the remains of the lost city of Vitcos and Espíritu Pampa. Macchu Pichu was probably not the Inca capital which Bingham believed it to be, but the location of the Incas' last refuge continues to fascinate an to draw expeditions into the area to the present day.

above

Hiram Bingham in *The Discovery of Machu Picchu*, *Harper's Monthly Magazine*, 1913:
'..suddenly we found ourselves in the midst of a jungle-covered maze of small and large walls, the ruins of buildings made of blocks of white granite, most carefully cut and beautifully fitted together without cement. Surprise followed surprise until there came the realization that we were in the midst of as wonderful ruins as any ever found in Peru. It seemed almost incredible that this city, only five days' journey from Cuzco, should have remained so long undescribed and comparatively unknown. Yet so far as I have been able to discover, there is no reference in the Spanish chronicles to Machu Picchu. It is possible that not even the conquistadors ever found this wonderful place.'

Sea

One of the earliest recorded sea voyages was that undertaken by Pharaoh Snefru around 3200 BC – ancient Egyptian records describe him as bringing 40 ships from Byblos to Phoenicia. The first recorded expedition was led by the Egyptian Hannu, who travelled from Egypt to the southern edge of the Arabian Peninsula (Punt) and the Red Sea in 2750 BC. Herodotus recorded that two millennia later, around 600 BC – 2000 years before Vasco da Gama – a three-year expedition sent by the Egyptian Pharaoh Necho circumnavigated the coast of Africa.

The Portuguese and Spanish later played important roles in sea exploration, leading the way to the New World and establishing trade routes along the coastline of Africa in the 15th and 16th centuries. The names of Columbus, of da Gama and of Magellan are firmly established in the history of this great age.

Latterly, within the photographic era, the 'exploration' of the sea has been not so much a geographical exploration, but rather a physical and psychological one, a testing of the limits of human endurance and of the human spirit.

Ann Davison, who became the first woman ever to sail across an ocean alone on her voyage from Plymouth to the West Indies in 1952, wrote: 'There were sunrises of such crystalline clarity and pristine glory that one could forgive any amount of travail for the joy of beholding those few golden moments when the world was born anew.'

Some took to the oceans for the adventure, others to prove a theory. In 1947, Thor Heyerdahl built the *Kon-Tiki*, a replica of an aboriginal balsa raft, to test his theories of how the Polynesians came to live on their South Pacific islands. With his companions, he left Peru and crossed 6,900 km (4,287 miles) to reach the Raroia atoll in 101 days, confounding sceptics who claimed his raft was not seaworthy and that the ancient Peruvians could never have reached Polynesia in this manner.

Chay Blyth, who with companion John Ridgway rowed across the Atlantic in an open boat in 1966, had a more prosaic reason. 'Why did I do it?' he reportedly said to an interviewer. 'Because at the end of my days, I'm going to be lying in my bed looking at my toes, and I'm going to ask my toes questions like "Have I really enjoyed life? Have I done everything I've wanted to do?" And if the answer is no, I'm going to be really pissed off.'

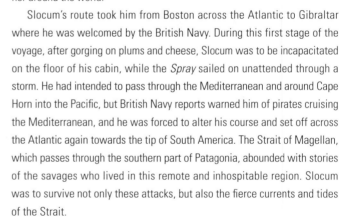
SAILING ALONE AROUND THE WORLD

The first man to complete the first circumnavigation of the world was a Canadian, Captain Joshua Slocum, at the very end of the 19th century. A retired master mariner and writer, Slocum was born in Nova Scotia, and had his first experience of sailing at the age of 14, when he ran away from home to work on a fishing schooner. Both sides of his family were sailors, passing on an instinct and love for the sea to him. As he says in his classic book, *Sailing Alone Around the World*, 'if any Slocum should not be found seafaring, he will at least show at least an inclination to whittle models of boats and contemplate voyages.'

Slocum took command of his first schooner at the age of 25, in San Francisco. For the next few years, he would sail the North-West coast, fishing, trapping, and building boats. But it was to be on his next charge, the bark *Washington*, that he would sail his first cross-Pacific trip to Australia where, in Sydney, he met the love of his life, Virginia Walker. In 1892, after captaining a number of boats, Slocum was offered a dilapidated 11-m (35-ft) old sloop named the *Spray* in a field; three years later, Slocum set off to sail her around the world.

Slocum's route took him from Boston across the Atlantic to Gibraltar where he was welcomed by the British Navy. During this first stage of the voyage, after gorging on plums and cheese, Slocum was to be incapacitated on the floor of his cabin, while the *Spray* sailed on unattended through a storm. He had intended to pass through the Mediterranean and around Cape Horn into the Pacific, but British Navy reports warned him of pirates cruising the Mediterranean, and he was forced to alter his course and set off across the Atlantic again towards the tip of South America. The Strait of Magellan, which passes through the southern part of Patagonia, abounded with stories of the savages who lived in this remote and inhospitable region. Slocum was to survive not only these attacks, but also the fierce currents and tides of the Strait.

From South America, Slocum caught the trade winds to the Islas de San Fernandez off Chile and then onto Samoa, with much of his journey spent reading in his cabin, letting the winds do all the work. A year and a half after his departure from Boston, he arrived in Newcastle, New South Wales to huge publicity. He beached the *Spray* for maintenance, and gave lectures and talks to raise money for his next leg. He returned to the sea, crossing the Indian Ocean, again capturing the trade winds, travelling via Mauritius, the rough Mozambique Channel and on to the Cape. In 1898 Slocum crossed his outbound track, completing the circumnavigation, and then continued home. After an absence of three years and two months and after 74,000 km (46,000 miles), Slocum and the *Spray* sailed into Fairhaven and to the point where the ship was first launched; 'I could bring her no nearer home,' he wrote.

Upon his return, Slocum was to further his other ambition – that of being a writer in the vein of authors such as Robert Louis Stevenson. Although he

right
'One midwinter day in 1892, in Boston, from where I had been cast up from old ocean, so to speak, a year or two before, I was cogitating whether I should apply for a command, and again eat my bread and butter on the sea, or go to work at the shipyard, when I met an old acquaintance, a whaling-captain, who said: "Come to Fairhaven and I will give you a ship. But," he added "she wants some repairs." … The ship turned out to be a very antiquated sloop called the *Spray*, which the neighbours declared had been built in the year 1.'

Joshua Slocum, *Sailing Alone around the World*

had already published, with his own finances, accounts of other voyages, the publication of *Sailing Alone around the World* in 1899 was to bring him both critical and financial reward.

At the age of 65, Slocum departed on his last journey. Planning to navigate the river Orinoco up to the Rio Negro and down the Amazon into the Atlantic, Slocum was to go missing and be legally declared dead as of 14 November 1909. Amidst tales of suicide, piracy and storms, his son Victor, also a sea captain, claimed it most likely he and his small boat were simply run down in crowded waterways.

Slocum remains an inspiration to all sailors, but following his circumnavigation, the feat was not attempted again for another two decades. He was followed by Harry Pigeon of the United States in 1921, Alain Gerbault of France in 1924 and Vito Dumas in 1942, who completed the journey totally within the southern hemisphere. It was 20 years more before another man was to attempt the challenge – this was Francis Chichester. His challenge was not only to complete the circumnavigation, but to beat the clipper ship times.

The clipper ships were originally designed to carry tea from the East and China to the United States and the United Kingdom. As tea leaves became mouldy in damp sea air, the trade in tea was a driver for a revolution in shipbuilding, with the clippers taking the place of the slower, stately East Indiamen, which carried tea for the East India company to the United Kingdom. The Clippers were fast and sleek with

right

With names like *Taeping*, *Ariel*, *The Caliph* and here, the *Cutty Sark*, the great square-rigged Clipper ships were the Concorde of their generation. Supremely elegant, lean and fast they carried a huge amount of sail and had sharp bows that sliced through the water. They began as the tea Clippers, bringing fame and wealth to their owners and captains as they raced – in one race up to 40 taking part – the 25,500 km (16,000 miles) to bring the first tea home from China to London in the mid-19th century. For the tea to be in the best condition – and therefore command the best prices – the journey time from the Orient was crucial. To meet the need, ships were specially built in British shipyards, although it is said they were developed out of the swift, manoeuvrable privateers built in America to raid British shipping during the War of 1812. When the trade shifted to the more reliable steam ships, the clippers instead took wool from Australia as their cargo.

much more sail, and the first true Clipper, the US-built *Rainbow,* in 1845, was so fast that she brought the news back first of her own record-time to Canton.

The arrival of the *Rainbow* sparked a race between the Americans and the British to build the fastest ships. The first crop of tea to reach the docks was guaranteed to get the best price, and this led to the annual China to London 'Tea Races', where the winner was the first to hurl its cargo on to the decks. Arguably, the greatest race was held in 1866, where after 25,500 km (16,000 miles) over 100-odd days, the boats were separated merely by a matter of minutes. After the clippers' own replacement by the steam ship, they were used to carry wool from Australia – these were the times Chichester aimed to beat.

Francis Chichester was born in 1901 in the United Kingdom, but emigrated to New Zealand at the age of 18, with only 10 pounds in his pocket. His interest in flight and travel began when he helped to establish an aviation company in Australia and then returned to England in 1925 and learnt to fly. In 1929, Chichester set off in a Gypsy Moth biplane for Sydney, Australia, becoming the second man to fly solo from England to Australia. Two years later, he became the first person to fly the Tasman Sea from east to west in his Gypsy Moth aeroplane fitted with floats, and was the first person to be awarded the Johnson Memorial Trophy for this epic flight.

After the Second World War, he took up ocean racing and in 1960 took part in the first-ever single-handed trans-atlantic race, which he won in 40 days, piloting *Gipsy Moth III*. In 1966 he set off single-handed aboard his 16-metre (53-foot) ketch, *Gipsy Moth IV*, to break the Clipper ship times and to set himself the task of rounding Cape Horn. It was a challenge that had been in his mind for many years, as he says in *Gipsy Moth Circles the World*:

The life of Sir Francis Chichester, one of the most remarkable British sailors, reads like an adventure story. While he will probably best be remembered for his sailing exploits, he had already notched up a series of achievements in the field of aviation before his voyage around the world in 1966–67 began an outstanding record of achievement that saw him simultaneously in the headlines and the record books. He is pictured here aboard *Gipsy Moth III* in 1964, aged 63.

'It not only scared me, frightened me, but I think it fair to say it terrified me … I told myself for a long time that anyone who tried to round the Horn in a small yacht must be crazy. Of the eight yachts I knew to have attempted it, six had been capsized or somersaulted before, during or after the passage. I hate being frightened, but even more, I detest being prevented by fright. The Horn had a fearsome fascination, and it offered one of the greatest challenges left in the world.'

As with Slocum's, Chichester's voyage was not without its heart-stopping moments. 3,700 km (2,300 miles) from Sydney, the boat's self-steering broke down and, worried that he would have to dock and have her fixed before Sydney, Chichester improvised and managed to right her. One day out of his journey from Sydney, *Gipsy Moth IV* capsized on a freak wave, throwing his cabin and provisions upside down. She had keeled over to 41 degrees below horizontal

On 29 January 1967 – the day after he was awarded his knighthood – Sir Francis Chichester left Sydney on the return leg of his round-the-world voyage via Cape Horn to the waters of Plymouth and home.

below

On his return home Sir Francis is said to have responded to the inevitable question, 'Why did you do it?' with the comment: 'Because it intensifies life.' After months with only his thoughts for company, the opportunity for a friendly wave from a passing vessel as he neared Plymouth on his round-the-world voyage was probably a moment to savour.

before righting herself, leaving Chichester wondering just what would happen if they were to meet a real storm. But it was rounding Cape Horn that was perhaps the most significant moment for Chichester; the target for which he had been aiming. Faced with winds measuring over 60 knots and 15-metre (50-foot high) waves and their resulting troughs, *Gipsy Moth IV*'s cockpit filled with water five times, invoking in him a feeling of utter helplessness. When he returned to Plymouth on 28 May 1967, he had logged 46,000 km (28,500 miles). Chichester was to continue to sail, but not in *Gipsy Moth IV*, of whom he said:

> '*Gipsy Moth IV* has no sentimental value for me at all. She is cantankerous and difficult and needs a crew of three – a man to navigate, an elephant to move the tiller and a 3'6" chimpanzee with arms 8' long to get about below and work some of the gear.'

Later in the year, Chichester was knighted by Queen Elizabeth. He died in 1972, two months after retiring from the Observer Single-Handed Trans-atlantic Race from ill-health. Fittingly, *Gipsy Moth IV* now resides next to the *Cutty Sark* in Greenwich, one of the most famous clipper ships.

Following Chichester's circumnavigation with only one stop, the next challenge was to complete the challenge non-stop. The following year with reports of four contenders to this challenge, the *Sunday Times* announced the Golden Globe trophy, whose participants included Chay Blyth and John Ridgway (see Ocean Rowing, p. 168), and which was eventually won by Sir Robin Knox-Johnston, who completed his solo non-stop circumnavigation in 312 days.

below

Ann Davison became the first woman to cross an ocean alone when, in 1952, she sailed from Plymouth to Antigua in the West Indies. She wrote that staying vigilant at all times was crucial to survival, but she also found time to write in lyrical terms about the intensity of the experience she found alone at sea: 'Conditions had a delicious dreamy Southern feel about them, calm and unhurried. There were lovely soft pearl-grey nights of a peculiar luminosity and soothing restfulness that were the physical manifestation of contentment.' The photo was taken in 1951, just prior to her departure from Plymouth.

WOMEN SAILORS

Until relatively recently, the world of competitive and round-the-world sailing has been almost a wholly male preserve. With few exceptions, women's names have not appeared in the annals of epic sea voyages or the sighting and naming of continents and new worlds. However, the stories of Mary Read and Anne Bonny, two notorious female pirates of the 18th century, and the following stories prove that women are no less capable of pushing back the frontiers of endurance, stamina and daring.

Being the first is always a uniquely awesome challenge. Ann Davison was the first woman ever to sail across an ocean alone. Back in 1952, she crossed the Atlantic from Plymouth to Antigua in the West Indies alone in her boat *Felicity Ann*, a mere 7 m (23 feet) long by 2.3 m (seven and a half feet) wide. A previous attempt in a much larger boat tragically claimed the life of her husband in a shipwreck.

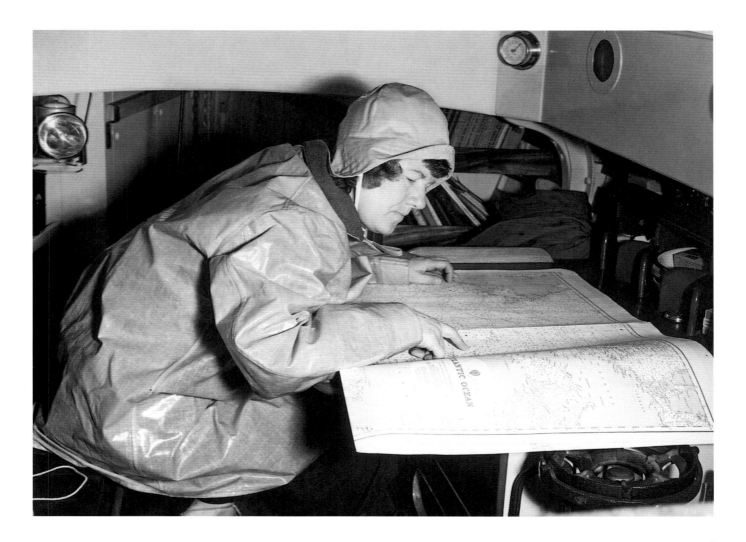

Her moving log of her voyage gives an insight into the reality of being aboard a small boat in the middle of a vast ocean — completely alone and constantly changing. On the leg out of Casablanca, she wrote:

'Then the air was breathless and there would not be the smallest sound from the ship, not even a creak, and the silence was primeval. One might have been alone on the planet where even a cloud spelt companionship. Most of the time, however, there was a huge swell in which *Felicity Ann* rolled abominably and flung her boom from side to side with a viciousness that threatened to wrench it clean out of its fastenings. She rattled her blocks and everything not immovably fast below with an aggravating irregularity, so that I was driven to a frenzy of restowing and rigging preventers in an effort to restore peace. An intermittent blop—rattle—crash on a small boat at sea is the nautical version of the Chinese water torture.'

above

Ann Davison called her book *'My Ship is So Small'* – and at 7 m (23 feet) long and just 2.3 m (7 feet) wide, its size underlines the enormity of taking on one of the world's mightiest oceans in such a tiny craft. Less than 10 years after the end of World War II, navigation and communication aids were rudimentary by comparison with today's high-tech equipment. The scale of the challenge she set herself was not only great at the physical level but also emotionally, as in a previous attempt to cross the Atlantic Ann lost her husband when their ketch was shipwrecked.

After Davison, the next challenge would be sailing round the globe single handed. The first woman to achieve this incredible feat was Poland's Krystyna Chojnowska-Liskiewicz. Born in Warsaw, Krystyna became a shipbuilding engineer at Gdansk before setting out on her record-breaking voyage in March 1967. Two years later she returned home in her yacht *Mazurek* where her feat was recognised with many decorations at home and abroad. She described her adventure in *Pierwsza dook ola Swiata* (*The First One Round the World*) in 1979.

To date, there have only been six recorded circumnavigations by women – proudly carrying the flags of nations from all around the world. In 1977–8 England's Naomi James circumnavigated; then France's Brigette Oudry sailed around the world south of the Great Capes. Ten years later Kay Cottee of Australia joined this exclusive club when she became the first woman to achieve a non-stop voyage from Sydney to Sydney in *First Lady* in 189 days.

left

Isabelle Autissier has made two complete circumnavigations: the BOC Challenge in 1990–91 and the Vendée Globe; and two half circumnavigations: the 1994–95 and 1998–99 BOC/Around Alone events. During the 1998–99 43,500 km (27,000-mile) solo race round the world, Autissier's 18-m (60-foot) yacht *PRB* capsized in what some sailors call the hole, the part of the Southern Ocean so remote that it cannot be reached by search-and-rescue aircraft. 3,000 km (1,900 miles) west of Cape Horn, deep within the zone of Antarctic drift ice, she was rescued by a fellow sailor, Giovanni Soldini of Italy.

right

Cape Horn lies at the tip of Patagonia and South America. Prior to the opening of the Panama Canal in 1914, Cape Horn was the route between North America's western ports and the Atlantic and Europe. It was discovered as a result of the Dutch East India Company's ban on any other Dutch trader using the Strait of Magellan to the north. Francis Drake had reported sailing further south many years earlier, and in 1615 two Dutch ships, the *Eendracht* and the *Hoorn*, sailed to find a new route. The *Hoorn*, named after the town which sponsored it, was lost to a fire, but the *Eendracht* carried on and discovered the passage, naming a highpoint on land, Cape Hoorn. This was later changed by the English to Cape Horn. The area is one of the most dangerous places to sail on the planet. This is because of the gale-force winds and huge waves which are created by the fast-flowing waters of the southern oceans being forced through the continents of Antarctica and South America.

Another French sailor, Isabelle Autissier, completed her first circumnavigation in 1990–91. Samantha Brewster set out from Southampton (UK) in October 1995 and completed the course in 161 days. A US record was set by Karen Thorndike who became the first American woman to sail solo around the world in her 11-m (36-ft) sloop *Amelia* between 1996 and 1998, starting and finishing in San Diego, California. She successfully challenged what are renowned to be the most treacherous waters on earth by rounding the five Great Capes: Cape Horn (tip of South America), Cape of Good Hope (South Africa), Cape Leeuwin (south of Perth, Australia), South East Cape (Tasmania) and Southwest Cape off New Zealand during her 53,000 km (33,000-mile) epic.

One of the most recent famous names in sailing is that of Ellen MacArthur. At 24, she became the fastest woman and youngest person ever to sail around the world, non-stop single-handed, beating the previous record by 10 days and finishing a close second in the formidable Vendée Globe race. Her utter determination – including living in a Portakabin for three years as part of her training – took her to the top of her chosen sport and she has become a a household name across the globe.

below

Ellen MacArthur returns to the south coast of England, February 15 2001, a few days after coming second in the Vendée Globe solo yacht race. Of her love and passion for living her life she says, 'A beautiful sunrise welcomed the day in … Inky black clouds slowly lit by an intense yellow sun … A very strong feeling of pleasure to be out here on the ocean … The sheer joy to race again, and the chance to be re-living this passion … I feel just lucky to be here.'

right

Ellen first went sailing at the age of eight with her aunt, and she was hooked enough that at school she saved up dinner money for three years to be able to buy herself her first boat – an eight-foot dinghy. At the age of 18, she had decided to become a professional sailor, and sailed single-handedly around Britain, and also became the youngest person to pass the Yachtmaster Offshore Qualification, achieving the highest possible marks in theory and practical examinations. In 1997 she took part in the Mini-Transat solo race across the Atlantic after buying *Le Poisson*, her yacht, which she refitted in France with no sponsorship, camped alongside in a tent. Her achievements brought her to the attention of the European retailer, Kingfisher, who have sponsored her since. In France, she was named 'La Jeune Espoire de la Voile' – 'Sailing's Young Hope'. She is pictured here after finishing the Vendée Globe.

below top

John Ridgway and Chay Blyth row into the Pool of London, two months after completing their 92-day epic crossing of the Atlantic. There to publicise their book *A Fighting Chance*, the story of that voyage, Ridgway said of rowing: 'I never liked it and I don't intend to do it again' and Blyth said, 'I never want to touch an oar again'.

below bottom

The journalists David Johnstone and John Hoare were lost at sea during their attempt to row the Atlantic. Seven men have died attempting to row the Atlantic: five British, one Russian and one American.

OCEAN ROWING

The first successful Atlantic row was completed by George Harbo and Frank Samuelson in 1896. Harbo and Samuelson were Norwegian immigrants working as fishermen in New Jersey. Discontented with their lot, they aimed to find fame and fortune by rowing across the Atlantic and cashing in by telling their story on the lecture-hall circuit; and so they bought a 5.5-m (18-foot) skiff, which they named the *Fox* after their sponsor, a New York newspaper editor. Despite capsizing twice and losing most of their provisions, they were to make the crossing in 55 days, which remained a record until Tom Mclean matched it on his solo row 90 years later. They were not to find the fortune that they expected, however, and both returned to fishing soon after.

Captain John Ridgway and Sergeant Chay Blyth of the UK became the second group to row the Atlantic, and the first this century. Ridgway had spent his childhood around boats and he was trained in seamanship and navigation by the age of 13, before joining the army and moving swiftly up its ranks. He was 26 when he responded to an advertisement seeking a partner to row across the Atlantic.

At the meeting, both Ridgway and David Johnstone, who had put out the advertisement, realised their incompatibility. Ridgway later said of Johnstone, 'He was a big bearded chap, a journalist. Quite overweight. I was proud of my fitness, and I didn't think this was somebody I'd want to row across the Atlantic with. So I decided to do it myself.' Ridgway's imagination had been captured, as he says in *A Journey to Ardmore*, 'After all the years of training, now there is reality, a chance to be fulfilled and make one joyous leap clear of time and the pettiness of life.'

Confident in his own abilities he set out to beat Johnstone's crossing, but with just a few months to go, Ridgway had no partner, no boat and no financing. He therefore decided to interview members of his own parachute regiment, and just a month and a half before the scheduled departure, Chay Blyth walked into Ridgway's office and offered his services. Ridgway had found his partner.

Chay Blyth grew up in Hawick, Scotland, far from the sea, and joined the army at 18, rising rapidly up the ranks. He and Ridgway had worked together a few times; Blyth had been Ridgway's platoon sergeant; they had trained in the Canadian Arctic together; and they had won a 24-hour army canoe race down the Thames. Although Blyth had never been to sea before, their ability to work as a team had already been tested, 'We were both aware of the paramount importance of not falling out with each other in mid-ocean,' Ridgway said.

Ridgway had aimed to depart at the same time as Johnstone and his partner, but Johnstone had rescheduled and Ridgway's own misfortune also

above

John Ridgway and Chay Blyth on board *English Rose III* on a ferry at Kilronan, Inishmore, following their landing on the west coast of Ireland. During the crossing, they had experienced immense storms and suffered from being almost constantly wet and cramped. The rowing placed enormous pressure on their hands and knees, and their cramped living compartments and salt irritating their skin added to the difficulties. During a particularly bad storm, they noted in their diary one night, 'We are completely in God's hands, at the mercy of the weather. All night the wind screams louder and louder and the sound of the sea becomes louder. We talked of many things, the night train to Scotland, the things we had done. And slowly we were overtaken by an enormous feeling of humility and the desire to return and try to live a better life.'

contributed: by the time Ridgway arrived in the USA, he had to be admitted to hospital because of blood poisoning. As he lay incapacitated on his back in a hospital bed, Johnstone and Hoare departed from Virginia Beach in their boat, The *Puffin*. Another two weeks would pass before Ridgway was sufficiently recovered to row, and on the evening of 4 June, 1966, they climbed aboard *English Rose III* and said their goodbyes.

The pair set out from Cape Cod into the Labrador current aiming for the Gulf Stream, initially both rowing and sleeping at the same time. They soon realised that much of the work and headway they were making during the day was being wasted at night, because of the strong currents. They hastily changed their plan, the men working as a pair for 12 hours each day and on alternate two-hour shifts each night. Very strong headwinds were a hindrance but these were to be merely child's play compared to the arrival of Hurricane Alma, the first hurricane to be spawned in the spring in over 60 years. For six hours, the men attempted to row and keep their course, while bailing out the water which swamped *Rosie* and making every effort to limit the damage being wreaked upon their provisions. They were hit by yet another powerful storm shortly after.

Blyth put their success and their ability to weather these storms down to the structure of command that they were a part of and were accustomed to. He later commented in an interview, 'John was an officer and used to giving orders, and I was a sergeant and used to taking them.' They considered their row as a survival exercise, just as they had worked in the desert or in the Arctic in the army, and they steadily became more efficient and effective.

Seventy days after their departure and with 1,450 km (900 miles) yet to go, Ridgway and Blyth had to restrict and ration their food supplies. Encountering an oil tanker on its way to South America, they were invited on board for fresh scrambled eggs, and restocked *Rosie* with supplies. Their position was 1,375 km (850 miles) from Land's End, and newspaper reports had apparently placed Johnstone and Hoare 1,200 km (750 miles) from Europe. The race was very much on.

After 91 days at sea, Ridgway and Blyth were within sight of the Aran Islands, off the coast of Ireland. They had danced with death and done the near-impossible, recalling the prediction they were given by the Coast Guard on their departure from America: a 95 per cent chance of dying. They were also to realise the flipside of that prediction by learning that the *Puffin* had been found upside down and Johnstone and Hoare had been lost at sea. The story of the fate of the two boats was to make national headlines.

Three years later, in 1969, John Fairfax of the UK was to become the first person to cross the Atlantic solo, and first to cross from east to west, from the Canary Islands to Florida. Fairfax had been inspired by Harbo and Samuelson, and had kept an account of their adventure under his pillow as a boy. Fifteen years later, his dream to row the Atlantic for himself was still alive in his mind.

right

Fairfax received a letter from Neil Armstrong, Michael Collins and Edwin A. Aldrin Jr after his row across the Atlantic: 'May we of Apollo 11 add our sincere congratulations to the many you have undoubtedly already received for your bold and courageous feat of rowing alone across the Atlantic. We who sail what President Kennedy once called "The new ocean of space" are pleased to pay our respects to the man who, single handedly, has conquered the still formidable ocean of water. We find it an interesting coincidence that you completed your arduous voyage here on earth at a spot very near the one from which we started our voyage to the moon. And that you arrived at your destination quite near the time that we reached ours. Yours, however, was the accomplishment of one resourceful individual, while ours depended upon the help of thousands of dedicated workers in the United States and all over the world. As fellow explorers, we salute you on this great occasion.' John Fairfax and Sylvia Cook are pictured here leaving the Gilbert Islands on their voyage from San Francisco to Australia.

above

John Fairfax was born in Italy during World War II to a Bulgarian mother and an English father. At the age of nine, on an Italian boy scout camping trip, he stole his leader's gun and sprayed the boy's hut with bullets. Soon after, he went to live in Argentina with his mother, but left home at 13 to go and live in the jungle; he wanted to 'live like Tarzan'. After living in San Francisco, he went back to Argentina, Guatemala and Panama; he then became a smuggler and pirate. Eventually tiring of the life, he moved to London where he prepared for his Atlantic row – an adventure he had thought of since his teenage years. It was during this time that he met his love, Sylvia Cook. Of her, he said: 'She proved to be a charming girl and a keen rower herself. I was definitely not her type, nor she mine, but in spite of this we liked each other, and after a while I forgot all the others and went out exclusively with her. As far as 1967 was concerned, she was the only bright light in my life.'

He began to train in earnest, his schedule consisting of a two-mile run in the morning followed by two hours of swimming and weight-lifting and then three or four hours of rowing on the Serpentine Lake in Hyde Park, London. At the same time, he was searching desperately for sponsors and funds. In response to a personal advertisement he put out in *The Times* of London, he received three useful replies. One was a cheque for £1, another was an offer of help to build the boat, and the other was from Sylvia Cook, who was later to become his girlfriend and sailing partner.

One hundred and eighty days after setting out from the Canaries, Fairfax and his boat *Britannia* arrived in Florida to a rapturous welcome. During the first few days of his crossing, Fairfax had questioned why he was going to sea alone. His next voyage was to be with Sylvia Cook, when they sailed and survived 12,750km (8,000 miles) across the Pacific together in 1971 their experiences including a shark attack.

The first solo row west to east across the Atlantic was to be achieved by another member of the British military, Tom Mclean, a member of the British élite force, the SAS. He had undergone the intense training of the SAS and seen active service in the Borneo jungle, but had no seafaring experience. He was 26 years old when he set out from St John's in Newfoundland in his 6-m (20-foot) dory *Super Silver* and crossed to Blacksod Bay in Ireland 70 days later.

Mclean went on to further the challenges of the Atlantic crossing by setting two records for sailing in the smallest boats. In 1982, he successfully crossed the Atlantic in a 3m (9" 9') boat and the following year, in one measuring 2.4m (7" 9') in length. In 1987 he regained the world record for the quickest crossing of the Atlantic, in 54 days. He also completed the crossing in a 11.2m (37-foot) bottle-shaped boat in 1990, and in 1996 in *Moby*, 'King of Whales', a whale-shaped, diesel-powered boat.

The Atlantic has since been crossed in a rowing boat over 80 times, in pairs, crews and solo. Patrick Quesnel was the first man to cross the Pacific single-handed, crossing from east to west in 1976. Gerard d'Aboville was the second to cross the Atlantic single-handed in 1980 after Tom McLean, and his imagination was captured. His confrontation with the Atlantic was to push him to attempt more and in 1991 he embraced the challenge of the Pacific, twice as wide and arguably considerably more dangerous. In 1991 he became the first man to row this ocean from west to east single-handed.

D'Aboville set out from Choshi in Japan in mid-July in *Sector*, an 8-m (26-foot) boat he designed and built. It consisted of a watertight living compartment, just 80 cm (31 inches) high, with a bunk, stove,

right

Tom Mclean designed and helped build this 11 m (37 ft) bottle- shaped boat, the *Typhoo Atlantic Challenger*, which he sailed from New York to Falmouth, England in 1990 over 37 days. The boat was powered by a diesel engine and furnished with a four-poster bed, and raised money for the National Children's Homes charity, a charity particularly personal to McCclean as he was an orphan himself.

below

Not content with rowing the Atlantic, in 1985, Tom McClean occupied Rockall to reaffirm Britain's claim on the small outcrop in the Atlantic. 450 km (280) miles west of the mainland, the 22 m (73 ft) high and 24 m (80 ft) wide rock has just one ledge of 3 m (10 ft) by 1.2 m (4 ft) near the summit. Mclean survived on this ledge for 40 days and nights in a unit of just 1.5 m by 1.2 m X 1.2 m (5 ft by 4 ft by 4 ft) that he designed himself. He also crossed the Atlantic in bottle-shaped and whale-shaped boats. McClean now runs an adventure centre on the west coast of Scotland.

radio, telex and a camera to film himself whilst rowing. What he was to encounter on his crossing would push him to the very limits of human endurance, both mental and physical. D'Aboville's departure had been delayed and as a result, he set off during one of the worst times of the year. Faced not only with the sheer physical challenge of rowing an average of 7,000 strokes per day, he was also faced with 12 m (40-foot) waves and 130-km (80-mile) per hour winds, culminating in a severe storm off the Oregon and Washington coast. His boat capsized 30 times, once for two hours where he was trapped inside, his oxygen depleting as he tried to right the boat. 134 days later, and almost three stone lighter, D'Aboville arrived at Illwaco, Washington.

left

In D'Aboville's account of his crossing, *Seul* (Alone), he discusses his attraction to the ocean and how, in crossing it and beating it, he went beyond the 'useful' drives and tasks of animals and achieved what only a human being could achieve: 'I have chosen the ocean as my field of confrontation, my field of battle, because the ocean is reality at its toughest, its most demanding. As my weapons against this awesome power, I have human values: intelligence, experience, and the stubborn will to win.'

right

In 1952, the French scientist, Dr Alain Bombard crossed the Atlantic in his rubber dinghy, *L'Hérétique*, (The Heretic) from the Canaries to Barbados. His aim was to prove that with no food or supplies, shipwrecked sailors could survive in an open boat living off the sea. During his 65-day crossing, he ate fish, plankton and seawater, losing 18 kg (three stone) as a result. He was awarded the Cross and Red Ribbon of the Legion of Honour by the French Minister of the Merchant Navy. The raft became compulsory cargo for all merchant and navy ships following his crossing. Bombard is pictured here on the right.

below

Thor Heyerdahl and Herman Watzinger chart the course of the *Kon-Tiki*, 28 December 1946 and so chart a course into history. There was by no means unanimous agreement over Norwegian Thor Heyerdahl's views on the origins of the Polynesian race and culture. To test his theory that they had originally come from the west and not the east as previously thought, he built a replica of an aboriginal balsa raft before setting out on a remarkable 101-day journey. Watzinger was Heyerdahl's second-in-command.

PROVING A THEORY – THOR HEYERDAHL

Thor Heyerdahl's motives for setting sail were altogether different from the other names in the story of man's understanding of the sea. Heyerdahl was a Norwegian zoologist, geographer and anthropologist who built three replicas of ancient sea craft in order to prove his migration theories.

Born in Larvik, Norway in 1914, Heyerdahl studied zoology and geography at university. As a student in 1937, he travelled to Tahiti with his wife Liv, where they studied the Polynesian culture and customs under the eye of the Supreme Polynesian Chief of Tahiti. They moved to the remote island of Fatu Hiva in the Marquesas Group, where they remained for a year, further studying the Polynesian customs and the origins of the island's plant life. His studies of plant life, prevailing winds and currents, and local legends and customs, pointed to the possibility that the island's inhabitants could have been settled from the east, from South America. Heyerdahl was to rock the scientific world and question established models with his theory that the islands had been settled in two waves, the first from Peru via Easter Island and the second via British Columbia. His theory was published in 1941 and more extensively in 1952 in his volume, *American Indians in the Pacific*.

Heyerdahl's work was met with strong resistance and scepticism from the geographical and anthropological communities, who maintained that migrants could not physically have travelled on their primitive craft. In 1947, to lend weight to his theory, Heyerdahl built a replica of the craft that South Americans used in ancient times. Despite a life-long fear of the ocean, he set sail from Callao, Peru with five other man on a boat named *Kon-Tiki*.

The *Kon-Tiki* consisted of a platform of 70 m² (750 ft²) with a cabin of bamboo and banana leaves, and two masts made of mangrove and was stocked up with native foods. Over 101 days they drifted 6,900 km (4,300 miles), adding

above

For most people the *Kon-Tiki* Expedition would have been enough excitement and adventure for one lifetime, but as Heyerdahl's research on ancient navigation continued, he became interested in reed boats made of papyrus. Again, conventional wisdom was that such craft would become waterlogged long before they were able to make substantial voyages. But in 1969 he constructed a vessel of ancient design from 12 tonnes of papyrus and, with a crew of seven, sailed *Ra* from Morocco some 4,350 km (2,700 miles) in 56 days until storms and problems with the construction forced them to abandon their attempt just seven days short of Barbados.

below

Spurred on by just missing his objective with the 15 m (49 ft) *Ra*, Heyerdahl was ready to repeat the voyage just 10 months later in the slightly smaller *Ra II*. Here they are shown setting off from Safi in Morocco, from where they sailed across the Atlantic at its widest part, completing the voyage to Barbados in just 57 days. Here was conclusive proof that simple vessels from the Mediterranean region could have crossed the Atlantic prior to Columbus – and how modern science had so underestimated ancient technology.

flying fish and plankton to their provisions. *Kon-Tiki* stayed afloat, and they arrived in Raroia in Polynesia, proving that the migration theory was possible. Heyerdahl wrote a book and made a film of the voyage, which won an Oscar for best documentary, captivating the public, but leaving many still sceptical. However, his later work found evidence of ancient navigation tools, increasing the acceptance of his views, and he began gradually to be taken more seriously.

Heyerdahl continued with his work on migration and ancient navigation, and in 1969, he built the *Ra*, a reed boat made of papyrus. The 15-metre (49 - foot) boat was launched from Safi, Morocco, and attempted to cross the Atlantic to show that boats could have been crossing the Atlantic prior to Columbus. With seven men from seven countries under the flag of the UN, the *Ra* was to sail 5000 km (3,125 miles), before being abandoned one week short of Barbados due to storms and construction problems. The following year, *Ra II* successfully crossed the widest part of the Atlantic (6,100km / 3800 miles) in 57 days, again proving that ancient vessels could make such a crossing.

In Iraq in 1977, Heyerdahl built the *Tigris*, this time aiming to show that civilisations in Mesopotamia, Egypt and the Indus Valley could have been in contact by sea. Wars in the area at the time prevented him from continuing, and he burnt the *Tigris* as an expression of anger at the political situation. Heyerdahl died at his home in Italy in 2001.

Underworlds

Even when the furthest shores and highest peaks had been identified, and in some cases reached or climbed, there remained frontiers as yet untouched by human exploration – the subterranean worlds of caves and the ocean floors.

It is thought that from earliest times man had used caves only for shelter, and so it is difficult to identify precisely the origins of caving purely for exploration. Shelter being the main consideration, early man was unlikely to have admired the underground world for its own sake – nevertheless, the painters at Lascaux, in France's Dordogne region, clearly penetrated further than was easy or necessary to find a place for their exquisite art, art that was created at least 15,000 years ago.

As recently as the 1970s a new tribe of people discovered in the Philippines were found to be living in caves but, in general, after man had learned to build houses, not only did he abandon caves, but these curious, mysterious openings into the earth took on a sinister aspect. Home to bats, silent creatures of the night, caves became enmeshed in legends in which they were seen as entrances to a dangerous underworld, perhaps even a gateway into hell itself.

Not until the 18th century did scientists begin exploring caves, albeit at first in a limited way, as lighting was difficult. Their reward was the discovery of the bones of extinct animals, which were claimed to prove that Noah's Flood really did happen.

Although scientific interest in the seas had begun as early as the 18th century, when Count Luigi Marsigli made observations of the salinity, temperature and currents of the Mediterranean, it was the spread of submarine telegraphy in the 19th century which really stimulated a need to understand the waves and currents of the deep sea floor. This coupled, with the publication of Darwin's *Origin of Species*, which sparked interest in marine biology, led to the voyage of HMS *Challenger*, which in 1872 set out on a three-year voyage, marking the birth of modern oceanography. Although human exploration of shallow waters was possible through diving, the true depths remained uncharted until the development in 1930 of a vessel strong enough to protect explorers from the immense pressure at the ocean floor – the bathysphere.

below

Édouard-Alfred Martel in 1890. In 1883, at the age of 24, Martel made the first scientific study of the Causses of south-west France, harsh, arid plateaux which beforehand had been little studied. His work on the study of the erosion of limestone made h m the acknowledged father of the science of speleology. His work was also of enormous benefit to the inhabitants of the region. The impoverished locals, seeking to force a living from the unforgiving landscape, had been prone to periodic bouts of life-threatening diseases as their water supplies became contaminated by poor sanitation. Martel was able to create a more hygienic water supply system. His writings on the area also encouraged the first tourists and so helped the locals improve their lives.

CAVING

Despite earlier visits for religious or exploratory purposes, most experts now date the science of speleology (the study of caves) to the late 19th century and the work of the Bohemian Adolf Schmidl, who explored the caves of Slovenia. His studies were expanded by others during the late 19th century, in particular by the Frenchman Édouard-Alfred Martel. Martel was born in 1859 and qualified as a lawyer, working as an attorney at the *Tribunal de Commerce* in Paris. But though the law was his livelihood, geology and travel were his loves, the two merging in an exploration of the cave systems of France, Italy, Germany, Spain and the United Kingdom. In June 1888 Martel visited a site at the base of Mont Aigoual in the Languedoc region of France where a river exploding from a rock fissure was known as *Bramabiau*, bellowing bull, because of the roar of water when the river was in spate. With the river level lowered by a dry summer Martel and his companions pushed past the waterfall at the mouth of the cave and, with difficulty, followed the river upstream. Over a two day period they explored 700 m (2,300 ft) of river course and a further 1,000 m (3,275 ft) of side galleries, eventually emerging on to the limestone *causse* where the river, the Bonheur, sank below ground. Martel had achieved the first following of a river from resurgence to sink. In 1895 he explored Marble Arch Cave in Northern Ireland and made the first descent of the 110 m (360 ft) main shaft of Gaping Gill in the English Pennines. The following year, together with Louis Armand, he explored the Cueva del Drach on Mallorca, discovering what was then the largest underground lake ever seen. In 1897 Louis Armand discovered a new sinkhole on the Causse Méjean, also near Mont Aigoual. When Armand and Martel explored it they discovered one of the most beautiful caves either had ever seen. On his return to the surface Martel said 'I came out as if from a dream'. Now open to the public, Aven Armand is considered the finest show cave in Europe, perhaps in the world. It has hundreds of beautiful formations including what is probably the world's tallest stalagmite.

Martel's books on caving included the first studies of hydrology, the basis of an understanding of cave formation. Though he was primarily a cave explorer, Martel was also interested in exploring any place where water met rock. He made the first exploration of the deep, tight gorge of the Verdon river in northern France, the path that now threads a spectacular way through the gorge being Sentier Martel. Martel died in 1938 at the age of 79.

Another great name from the early history of modern caving is the Habsburg Baron von Czoernig-Czernhausen who explored the caves around Salzburg as well as others in Europe. When the Baron died, at the age of 62, he

is said to have been buried at night by the light of miners' lamps and close to Untersberg beneath which he had spent many happy hours. His passion for the area was rewarded after his death when a local cave, Lamprechtsofen, which until recently held the title of the world's deepest cave, was named after him.

A contemporary of the Baron, Norbert Casteret, is another great figure of early caving. Like Martel, Casteret was French, but concentrated his efforts on the vast caves of the Pyrenees. Casteret discovered several caves decorated with prehistoric paintings, and also the oldest known sculptures, clay models of a bear and a lion, in Montespan in France's Haute-Garonne. In Montespan in 1922 Casteret dived a sump – a sump is where a river completely fills a cave passage, forcing the caver who wishes to continue exploration to dive in search of an airspace on the far side. Holding his breath Casteret explored the sump. Édouard-Alfred Martel, then aged 63, had been astonished by this dive, writing that it was of 'unparalleled daring …. (Casteret) plunged under a submerged ceiling into the shadows of an underground river, braving a tunnel whose length he could not know'. Though there had been attempted dives before Casteret's, they had been infrequent and unsuccessful, the divers being lucky occasionally to escape with their lives. Casteret's dive brought the technique of free-diving (diving without apparatus) during exploration fully into the evolving sport of caving, though it is still usual to explore sumps with breathing apparatus first to discover their length. Casteret was also involved in the explorations of the Pierre Saint-Martin system in 1952–3 which resulted in its claiming the title of world's deepest cave.

right

Major caves may be
discovered in unlikely
places. By digging out a
series of short, mud-
filled caves named Ogof
Draenen – the Cave of
Thorns – in South
Wales, in 1994 a group
of cavers broke into a
series of massive,
ongoing passages. Taken
within days of its
discovery, this
photograph shows part
of the main streamway
named Beyond a Choke
(a typical cavers' pun: a
'choke' is a boulder-filled
section of passage).
Ogof Draenen has been
mapped to over 63 km
(41 miles) long and is
now considered one of
the top caves of the
world – a significant find
in recent years.

The Columns in Ogof Fynnon Ddu are found in the upper reaches of the cave, which contains one of the finest streamways in Britain. The resurgence area first received a serious investigation in 1942 and became one of the earliest sites dived by the fledgling Cave Diving Group, but the main part of the cave was only discovered as part of a wave of exploration in South Wales during the 1960s.

THE DEEPEST, THE LONGEST

The record for deepest point reached in a cave was first established in Italy in 1841 when man for the first time reached 305m (1000 ft) below the surface. This was increased to 689 m (2261 ft) in the Pierre Saint-Martin in 1953. Pierre Saint-Martin has an almost mythical status among cavers, aided by the fact that it has entrances in both France and Spain, the cave burrowing under the border between the two countries. Its exploration was the work of the top cavers of the day, most notably Casteret. Ironically, as Casteret's team was reaching its deepest, point another Frenchman, Jo Berger, was discovering the entrance to a cave that would overtake Pierre Saint-Martin as the site holding the world's depth record. Exploration of Gouffre Berger, on the Vercors plateau at Grenoble, went beyond the 1000 m (3,275 ft) mark in 1956, ultimately reaching 1,135 m (3,725 ft). By 1966 Pierre Saint-Martin had regained the record, but Gouffre Berger remained a cherished prize among cavers. That fact and the dangers of the sport, were illustrated

when, in 1987, a 17 year old British caver went into the cave and disappeared. Exhaustive searches failed to find any trace of him and increasingly fantastic rumours spread about his disappearance. Only a year later was the mystery finally solved when a previously unexplored gallery was entered and the young man's body found. Mercifully it appears that he probably died instantly in a fall: a lingering death, trapped and in total darkness, is a fear which all extreme cavers must set aside before they descend.

The Pierre Saint-Martin system reclaimed the record with 1,321m (4,334 ft) before another French cave, Réseau Jean-Bernard in the Haute-Savoie, first discovered in 1964, took the record beyond 1,500 m (4,925 ft) in 1983. This cave in turn was replaced by the Gouffre Mirolda, also in the Haute-Savoie of France, in which cavers went beyond 1,600m (5,250 ft), over a mile underground. Austria's Lamprechtsofen took the record a little further in the 1990s, but that record requires an understanding of the way in which depths are measured in caves, as those entering Lamprechtsofen were travelling uphill rather than down. Some caves are entered at resurgences (where the stream which carved the cave reaches the surface again). If the cave is entered at the point where the water sinks, then the caver is following the water downwards, but the caver follows the stream upwards if the resurgence is used to gain access. Cave depths are therefore measured as the distance between the highest and lowest points. In the case of Lamprechtsofen, the cavers at the maximum 'depth' were actually above their entrance (and fairly close to the point at which the carving stream disappeared underground). Today the record depth is held by a Georgian cave. Originally called Voronya, the cave's name has recently been changed to Krubera, as it was later discovered that the system had already been given that name.

There are now well over 400 caves throughout the world with depths of over 500 m (1640 ft) – the deepest in Britain is Ogof Ffynnon Ddu in South Wales at just over 300 m (985 ft), more than 50 of these descending beyond 1000m

right
At over 560 km (350 miles) long, Mammoth Cave in Kentucky, USA, is the longest known cave in the world and, with Optimisticheskaja in the Ukraine lying in second place at 212 km (133 miles), it seems likely that Mammoth will retain its record for many years. Mammoth's exploration dates from the 19th century, when black slave guides showed tourists around the cave. Further exploration is certain to extend the system still further.

above
Dan yr Ogof was first explored in 1912 by the Morgan brothers, who used a coracle to cross deep pools near the entrance to the cave. Explorations in 1937 and again in 1966 eventually entered some stunningly beautiful passages, including Cloud Chamber where delicate stalactites termed straws (named as they are hollow) festoon the ceiling. The cave is today over 15 km (9 miles) long.

(3,275 ft), a mark which was passed for the first time less than 50 years ago.

Though Krubera is the deepest cave, it is not the longest in terms of the length its galleries, that being the Mammoth Cave System in Kentucky, USA where the present surveyed length exceeds 560 km (350 miles). This is almost 10 times longer than the longest cave in Britain, the Ease Gill System in the Yorkshire Dales which now exceeds 70 km (44 miles).

CAVE DIVING

After Casteret's free dive in 1922 there were significant attempts at diving using specialised and 'hard hat' diving equipment in Swildon's Hole and Wookey Hole in England's Mendip Hills in the 1930s by Graham Balcombe and his associates. Such equipment was cumbersome in the tight environment of caves, particularly as the heavy suits and compressors had to be taken down to the sumps, not always a feasible proposition. Cave diving did not really take off until Cousteau's work on self-contained breathing apparatus allowed cavers to dispense with these. Not surprisingly Cousteau's invention was first taken up by a Frenchman, Guy de Lavaur, whose book *Caves and Cave Diving* remains a classic. The use of sub-aqua equipment, often with teams of 'sherpas' to stow spare air bottles at strategic points, has allowed cave divers to make increasingly long dives. In Florida and the Bahamas dives of over 10 km (6.25 miles) have been made (utilising air pockets), with continuous dives in excess of 3 km (the current longest is 'O' Tunnel in Florida's Wakulla Springs which is 5506 m (18,064 ft) long). There is, however, a very great difference between diving in the clear, warm waters of Florida and the cold, murky

left
Richard Stevenson preparing to dive in Chamber 3 of Wookey Hole, a cave beneath England's Mendip Hills. Wookey is another fine show cave, but extends far beyond the last point reached by visitors, large sections of the cave then being underwater. The photograph gives an impression of the complexity of equipment necessary to dive such systems.

waters of Britain and other European countries and these need to be borne in mind when comparing dives.

For that reason many point to the through dive which linked Keld Head and Kingsdale Master Cave in Yorkshire, England as a major landmark in the sport. The link, 1,830 m (6,000 ft) without air pockets, was made in January 1979 by Geoff Yeadon and Oliver Statham, but only after many months of exploration involving several other divers. One of these was the German Jochen Hasenmayer who on one dive got off route when a guide line became slack during his exit from one section of the flooded passage. Yeadon dived to find the missing German, discovering him trying to force his way through a slot that was far too small. To reassure Hasenmayer, Yeadon put his hand through the slot. In almost zero visibility Hasenmayer took the hand, Yeadon commenting later that he had been convinced he was 'shaking a dead man's hand'. But despite the German's air being almost exhausted, Yeadon was able to shine his light through the correct hole and thus help Hasenmayer around the obstacle. This part of the passage is still called Dead Man's Handshake.

THE FUTURE

The early cavers, Martel and his companions and others from the same period, used candles or miners' lamps to explore, the use of carbide lamps, in which acetylene gas is created and then burnt, making a much more compact light available from the 1900s. Comparable electric lights became available from the 1940s. Early ladders were of rope, with wooden rungs, but from the late 1930s 'electron' ladders of lightweight wire, on which equally lightweight rungs were swaged, became available. Though modern cavers now use wetsuits or fleece undersuits to keep them warm when wet and modern boots which are warmer and lighter, oversuits are still used (especially in Europe) to guard against abrasion and a special helmet to protect the head. Rope techniques, some borrowed from climbing, others developed or refined within the sport, have allowed rapid descents and ascents of drops which have reduced the times for great depths to be reached.

Whereas, in climbing, the highest peaks are known, the steepest faces discernible, in caving there is no ultimate cave, merely the advancement of records by dogged exploration: the longest, the deepest caves may yet be discovered. As a consequence caving is a more democratic sport than climbing. There are no genuine international stars in the caving world, the exploration of systems usually being the work of local groups who, over a period of months or years, extend the limits of a particular system. That, together with the often magnificent views of stalagmites and stalactites, makes exploring the underground world a fascinating activity.

below
Mapped to over 70 km (110 miles) long the Ease Gill System in the northern Pennines is the longest known cave in the British Isles and comprises a series of caves that have been explored (or 'pushed' in cavers' parlance) and linked together. This beautiful stalactite-filled chamber is named Straw Gallery. The formations are formed by the accretion of calcite (calcium carbonate) from the water dripping from the roof of a cave. Stalagmites grow upwards from the cave floor, while stalactites grow downwards from the roof. Occasionally the two meet to form columns of calcite.

BEEBE, BARTON, PICCARD, COUSTEAU

In 1930, two men in a 1.4-m (4.5-foot) wide hollow steel ball dived 435 m (1,426 ft) into the Bermudan sea attached by a steel cable to a ship above. William Beebe and Otis Barton, peering out through round quartz windows, looked out on to what had never been seen before – the deep ocean.

William Beebe, scientist, writer, explorer and visionary, was born in Brooklyn, New York in 1877 and, studying and tracking rare birds for the New York Zoological Park, he travelled widely, including the Far East and the Galapagos Islands. He had subsequently become involved in the marine environment and was frustrated by his inability to descend into the deep and study the life there. Barton, similarly, was fascinated with the natural world, and searched out fossils, rare animals and deep-sea creatures. It was, however, more his training and talents as an engineer that were to combine with Beebe's vision to become the stuff of legends.

In 1928, Beebe was already a public figure, having written many popular works, and was therefore receiving countless letters offering assistance for various crackpot schemes to pursue his challenge of the deep. One of these letters was from a young Barton, complete with comprehensive calculations and blueprints for a spherical diving craft. Beebe named this craft the bathysphere, from the Greek for deep (*bathus*) and its spherical shape.

The finished bathysphere weighed 2,270 kg (5,000 lbs), a practical consideration for the ship that would have to carry her and winch her up from the seabed. Keeping its weight down, however, meant that the space inside, which would carry both Barton and Beebe, would be minimal. Entry to the bathysphere was through a

Prior to the inventions of Beebe, Barton, Piccard and Cousteau, divers had used bells or helmets in which to capture air and explore under the surface of the sea. In the 1920s, before the bathysphere, Beebe said 'Don't die without having borrowed, stolen or made a helmet of sorts, to glimpse for yourself this new world.' Barton had thought the same: as a young boy, he had explored his local harbour in Massachusetts by fashioning a wooden box with glass windows to act as a helmet. Weighed down with rocks and sandbags, he breathed air forced into the helmet via a bicycle pump. Barton is seen here inside the bathysphere in 1930, showing just how cramped conditions were.

38-cm (15-inch) opening, which, once the men were inside, would be sealed up with ten steel bolts, the weak spot in a craft whose walls were 3.8cm (1.5 inches) thick. Opposite the door were three round quartz windows, jutting out from the bathysphere to take account of the extra thickness the material would require under such pressure. Cables containing telephone wire linked Beebe and Barton to the crew above.

This dive to 435 m (1,426 ft) was followed by many other dives, breaking a new record some months later at 670 m (2,200 ft) and another in 1934 to 923 m (3,028 ft). Beebe was to publish accounts of his dives, including details of some of the marine life he had seen, but much of this met with resistance in the scientific community. Many claimed that the creatures Beebe described were simply the product of an overactive imagination, or cited the thickness of the viewing quartz as a hindrance to any truly objective and scientific identification of deep-sea life.

above

'To climb the highest peaks, to travel through … celestial space, to turn our searchlights upon eternal darkness, that is what makes life worth living', said Auguste Piccard, the creator of *Trieste*. Although a robot explored Challenger Deep years later, no living person has returned there since the *Trieste*. Following its epic descent, the craft was no longer considered safe and was taken out of service. Cousteau told Auguste Piccard, 'Professor, your invention is the most wonderful of this century.' The picture shows Dr Andreas Rechnitzer and Jacques Piccard.

above right

As radio signals are swallowed by the sea, communication with the bathysphere was via copper wires that connected to the surface ship. More recent deep-sea communications have involved transmitting sound waves which can travel much further, though slower than light. Seeing deep beneath the surface was also a problem due to water particles scattering and dissipating light. Even the most powerful searchlights cannot penetrate much more than 20 metres in the deep sea.

But Beebe's writings certainly did serve as a source of inspiration for many, and rightly expressed the sense of wonder that this new technology aroused. As he described in *Half Mile Down*, the exploration of the sea was akin to that of space in its removal from everyday life:

'The only other place comparable must surely be naked space itself, out far beyond [the] atmosphere, between the stars, where sunlight has no grip upon the dust and rubbish of planetary air, where the blackness of space, the shining planets, comets, suns, and stars must really be akin to the world of life as it appears to the eyes of the awed human being, in the open ocean, one half mile down.'

Beebe expected new technologies rapidly to supersede his craft, but the absence of any significant commercial benefits and the onset of World War II contrived to lessen interest in such deep-sea diving. Barton would build a new, stronger craft called the benthoscope in 1949, with which he descended to 1,370 m (4,500 ft), but essentially, the need for a cable linking it to the boat above was restricting deeper descents. Whilst Beebe's and Barton's efforts were important and ground-breaking, they were but a drop in the ocean; the deepest depression of the world's oceans was 10,900 m (35,800 ft) down. Challenger Deep, so called because of the British boat which discovered it, was the deepest point of the Marianas Trench, a 2,550 km-long (1,600 mile) depression in the Pacific Ocean, off the coast of Guam.

This Everest of the seas was to be broken by Jon Walsh and Jacques Piccard, in the *Trieste* – a bathyscaphe. The *Trieste*'s ability to traverse these 10,900 m (35,800 ft) was given by its new method of descending and ascending the ocean. Whereas the bathysphere and benthoscope had relied upon a winch for their movement, the *Trieste* relied upon an upper float. Based on the principle of a balloon, its cabin was a steel sphere capable of withstanding the massive pressure at this depth. When the pilot wanted to

On land, we experience a pressure of one atmosphere, the weight of the earth's atmosphere. Underneath the ocean's surface, each 10 m (33 feet) descended adds 1 more atmosphere. In the deepest part of the ocean, nearly 11 km (7 miles) down, the pressure is 1,200 atmospheres or 1,250 kg per square cm (18,000 pounds per square inch). Any diving craft (such as the *Trieste*, pictured here) filled with air is subjected to this immense pressure and must be built to withstand it. Fish that live at these depths do not implode under the weight as they are filled with water at the same compression.

descend, the air-filled tanks at the ends of the float were flooded with seawater; to float back up, iron pellets were released. To fine-tune the descent, the pilot could release gasoline — less dense than water — from a central reservoir and allow water to flow in.

The bathyscaphe was designed by Auguste Piccard, Jacques's father, who piloted its early dives himself. A physicist by training, Piccard worked with Einstein on the study of cosmic rays, which in 1931 led him to take a hydrogen-filled balloon 15,250 m (50,000 ft) up into the atmosphere. Though this broke existing records, Piccard was not satisfied and went on to ascend to 17,000 m (55,800 ft). He was later to say that this pioneering technology actually evolved from his early ideas for the bathyscaphe and it was also important to the later development of space exploration.

On 23 January, 1960 Jacques Piccard and Don Walsh began their descent. At its terminal velocity, the *Trieste* travelled at a metre (three feet) per second, reaching 8,200 m (27,000 ft) in roughly three hours. They reached the floor of the Trench at one o'clock, the Trieste's 13-cm (five-inch) thick steel walls withstanding a pressure of 1.5 tonnes per square cm (nine tons per square inch) ; more than 99 per cent of the world's oceans lay above them. Since that successful journey to the base of the world, no man has ever been back.

The principal drive for these deep-sea craft had always been the desire to discover the plant and animal life that existed at these depths. Whilst their invention allowed man to go deeper than he had

below

Cousteau is shown here on board *Calypso* with his diver, Albert Falco. Calypso was a retired World War II minesweeper which Cousteau had adapted for his oceanic exploration. It was whilst on *Calypso* on the Red Sea that Cousteau is said to have come up with the idea of what became the *Soucoupe*, 'Throw the classic idea of submarines out the window,' he said 'and start with what we need.'

below right

Cousteau was also something of an artist and poet, expressing his love of the ocean through his many photographs, films and writings. Of being underwater he wrote, 'From birth, man carries the weight of gravity on his shoulders ... but man has only to sink beneath the surface and he is free. Buoyed by water, he can fly in any direction – up, down, sideways – by merely flipping his hand. Underwater, man becomes an archangel.

ever been before, they were very restrictive in terms of their manoeuvrability; an important consideration for scientists who truly wanted to explore. It was Jacques-Yves Cousteau who perhaps contributed most to this particular form of undersea exploration. In the 19th and early 20th century, divers were limited, like the bathysphere, by tethers and hoses linking them to an air supply, and by the 1930s compressed air was being used, but its application meant short and shallow dives. Cousteau and his group of divers were already affording divers more freedom through their invention of fins and goggles, but Cousteau's development of the Aqua-Lung was to revolutionise its practice.

Cousteau carried out the majority of research for the Aqua-Lung during World War II, when he was employed by French Naval Intelligence. Obtaining permission from the occupying forces to shoot cultural films in the Mediterranean as a cover, Cousteau was actually developing a self-contained underwater breathing system. With German and Italian forces using military frogmen in the war, his first model was tested in the strictest secrecy and the group went on to use it for dives of between 50 and 100 feet. At this time, the mixture of gas used – nitrogen and oxygen – brought about the 'rapture' of the depths, where nitrogen in the blood induces feelings of drunkenness and tiredness, something which they experienced as they tested the apparatus at greater and greater depths. Pushing the equipment to its

limits brought the death of one of their team, Maurice Fargues, who reached 120 m (396 ft) before they lost touch with him, later finding him with his mouthpiece dangling at his chest. Despite this tragic loss, the Aqua-Lung had set the standard for future diving systems.

After the war, and during the time that Piccard was developing the *Trieste*, Cousteau, frustrated with the limits of scuba diving, was approaching deep-sea exploration craft from a different angle. Although the bathyscaphe had proved its ability to reach the deepest of depths, its weight and design meant that it lacked the power of manoeuvrability, something which the true exploration of the undersea world vitally required. Cousteau, whilst on board his ship *Calypso* on the Red Sea, began to shape his ideas for a new deep-sea diving craft.

With his prerequisites being that it needed to be light enough to carry on Calypso, and that it needed to carry two people, Cousteau came up with the shape of a flattened ball for this new craft. It was to move like 'angels' he said, the way his Aqua-Lung had allowed divers to move, and it also made use of the lessons learned in the building of the bathyscaphe. The new vehicle, the 3-metre long (nine-foot) *Soucoupe* weighed just four tons, its pilots lay on their stomachs to peer out of larger windows: it had cameras and lights attached and it had a claw to collect specimens. Soucoupe became the prototype of all modern undersea research vehicles and was capable of withstanding pressures that conventional submarines would have collapsed under. The *Soucoupe* began diving in 1959 and was in service for over three decades.

Index